THE KOSHER-COOKBOOK TRILOGY

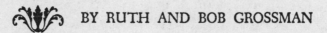 BY RUTH AND BOB GROSSMAN

Galahad Books • New York City

Library of Congress Catalog Card Number: 76-3400
ISBN: 0-88365-150-5
Published by arrangement with Paul S. Eriksson, Inc
Manufactured in the United States of America
Designed and illustrated by Arouni.

INTRODUCTION

When Grandma set down the first recipe that was later to grow into *The Chinese-Kosher Cookbook*, *The Italian-Kosher Cookbook* and *The French-Kosher Cookbook*, little did she realize what she was getting into. Almost overnight she became the sensation of Bensonhurst, a neighborhood deep in the heart of Brooklyn, famous for its stoop-sitting marathons.

Neighbors called for advice on how to fold a won-ton or flip a crêpe; she was asked to sign autographs at the local bookshop; the grocer wanted to know what was this "soy sauce" everybody was asking for; and suddenly the family circle grew into a three-ring circus with all the relatives clamoring for free copies. At first, Grandma was very generous and gave away dozens of books. But as more were published the bookkeeping became very confusing and Grandma was even getting requests from relatives she thought were still in Poland.

"Everybody wants for free. But believe me, with all the *shnorras* in our family you could spend a fortune being nice."

So we had a meeting in the publisher's office ("not even a piece cake they're serving") to see if all three cookbooks could be put into one volume. This way Grandma wouldn't have the *kupdraynish* of remembering who had what book.

When we told Grandma that the name of the new book was *The Kosher-Cookbook Trilogy*, she was heard to remark as she had once before, "*As men lebt, d'lebt men alles.*"

Ruth and Bob Grossman

Brooklyn Heights, New York

THE CHINESE-KOSHER COOKBOOK

THE CHINESE-KOSHER COOKBOOK

 BY RUTH AND BOB GROSSMAN

*To Grandmother Slipakoff
who held her first pair of
chopsticks at eighty*

Thou shalt not eat any abominable thing . . .

And every beast that parteth the hoof, and cleaveth the cleft into two claws, and chewest the cud among beasts, that ye shall eat . . .

These ye shall eat of all that are in the waters: all that have fins and scales shall ye eat . . .

Of all clean birds ye shall eat . . .

But these are they of which ye shall not eat: the eagle, the ossifrage and the osprey . . . and the glede, and the kite, and the vulture after his kind,

And every raven after his kind . . .

And every creeping thing that flieth is unclean unto you: they shall not be eaten . . .

But of all clean fowls ye may eat . . .

Ye shall not eat of any thing that dieth of itself . . . thou shalt not seethe a kid in his mother's milk . . .

DEUTERONOMY XIV

PREFACE

Friday night is a big night in a Jewish home. It is the beginning of the Sabbath and it is usually the time when that part of the family which has moved away, through marriage, or a desire to live a bachelor's existence in the Big City, is cajoled and coerced to "come over, you should have a nice, hot meal with the family."

But after being exposed to the epicurian delights of some of the most wonderful restaurants in the world, we began to hesitate about the delicious, but routine chicken or roast beef of Friday night. Ruth's grandmother (who lives in Louisiana, of all places!) cooks exactly the same dishes in exactly the same manner as Bob's grandmother (who lives in Brooklyn, of all places!). So no amount of, "What's the matter, you forgot maybe the address?" or, "You can bring even the poodle if he stays already under the table," could deter us from our favorite food at wonderful Chinese restaurants we had discovered all over the world . . . from Hong Kong to Tel Aviv.

So one day, Grandmother Slipakoff said, "All right, you'll come over Friday night, I'll cook Chow Mein."

We went over that fateful evening, more out of admiration for Grandma's sense of humor than with anticipation of having a Chinese meal . . . we knew we'd get chicken or roast beef or even chopped liver served with a Chinese name. But what to our wondering eyes should appear but Grandma's first attempt at acknowledging the 20th Century! Won Ton Soup ("so good the *Rebitsen* could eat it")—Jewish Chow Mein, and for dessert, the age old Chinese restaurant favorite: pineapple chunks pierced with toothpicks.

Grandmother Slipakoff, now 82, has a favorite Jewish expression: "*As men lebt, d'lebt men alles.*" (As I live, I see everything.) And we felt we'd seen everything. So Grandmother Slipakoff got everyone she could—the neighbors, her own children, the seltzer man— to collect Chinese recipes . . . and with her great natural talent as a cook, she figured out a way to make her grandchildren's favorite dishes Kosher, so she could cook them and there'd be no excuse for our not coming over to dinner each time we were asked.

We still enjoy the traditional Jewish dishes we grew up with . . . but we know the world of Jewish cooking will never be the same. We thought we'd truly seen everything, until one day: Grandma asked us to take her to Chinatown . . . and there, as we stood in back of a little shop with our mouths open in amazement, Grandma Slipakoff bought two pairs of chopsticks . . . one *fleischig* . . . and one *milchig!*

Truly: *As men lebt, d'lebt men alles!*

Ruth & Bob Grossman

Brooklyn Heights, N. Y.

TABLE OF ✿ CONTENTS

THE CHINESE-KOSHER COOKBOOK

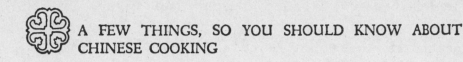

A FEW THINGS, SO YOU SHOULD KNOW ABOUT CHINESE COOKING

There are a few things, that maybe you should know, so you can be a real "mayvin" of Chinese cooking.

First and most important is timing. This doesn't mean you have to break your neck, rushing around the kitchen. It just means that you've got to think ahead.

The ingredients you use are sliced nice and thin, or chopped up fine so they cook nice and even all over and also fast. You'll be smart if you prepare all ingredients before you even put a pot on the stove. These you can put in little bowls so they'll be ready when you need them. This will prevent all the "tsurris" of burning food and sliced thumbs. (You shouldnt know from it!)

Most of the recipes that you'll see in this book will call for a little frying. This doesn't mean regular frying, it means what they call in Hong Kong, "stir-frying." A little oil you should put in the frying pan and when it's good and hot, then you can throw in the ingredients. Keep high the fire and just fry and stir, fry and stir, fry and stir. In a minute or two it'll be done. This trick keeps the food from burning and makes sure that all the pieces are evenly cooked. It also is very healthy, you don't soak out the vitamins and all the healthy juices are sealed in.

Deep-frying is already another method of preparing Chinese food. For this, a deep-fryer, or just a pot oil will be perfect. For a rule of "sliced" thumb, when the oil bubbles a little it's about right for fish and chicken. When it smokes, then it's good for beef.

Also, we shouldn't forget to tell you, peanut oil or other vegetable oil is very good to fry in. (And it's Kosher yet!)

When the recipe calls for meat, make sure it's good and lean— not that fat stuff the butcher tries to get rid of. If you need sliced

3

meat, the best thing to do is to freeze the meat a little. This will make it easy to cut into thin slices. When you're through slicing, they should measure about 2″ x 1″ and be ⅛″ thick. When the recipe calls for slivers or shreds, then you can cut the meat into pieces like matchsticks. Another thing to remember, always cut against the grain. Also, you should cut off all the gristle.

Onions and mushrooms cut straight. Other vegetables cut a little slanty. When you cut slanty, each piece has more surface open and you'll see already how much faster it cooks.

Most of the items used in these recipes you know. Other things, like soy sauce, which is made from soy beans and is brown and salty, might be new to you; but you shouldn't be without it! This, together with bamboo shoots, water chestnuts, and bean sprouts you can find in almost any supermarket. MSG, which is monosodium glutamate, is used to bring out the "tamm" in all foods. It is a white powder made from wheat flour. It's sold under a lot of different brand names. (Listen, it's wonderful even when you're not cooking Chinese food.)

You'll see in these recipes duck sauce and mustard. Duck sauce, so you shouldn't worry, doesn't have duck in it. It contains peaches, apricots and other fruits with vinegar, salt, sugar and spices. You'll find it in any grocery; and mustard you'll mix yourself from a little dry mustard and water.

So Mazeltuv! Now you know a few things about Chinese cooking. You should live and be well!

YOU'RE USING MAYBE CHOPSTICKS?

This maybe will help you get the idea. First you should place one chopstick in the round hollow between your thumb and your index finger and rest its lower end below the first joint of the third finger. This chopstick doesn't move. Hold the other chopstick between the tips of the index and middle fingers, making steady its upper half against the bottom of the index finger, using the tip of the thumb to keep it already in place. To pick up things, move the upper chopstick with index and middle fingers. So your food shouldn't get cold while you're learning, maybe practice with the forshpeis. Have plenty of napkins—and plenty guests with a good sense of humor.

Zei Gezint!

5

FORSHPEIS

TEA EGGS OY VAZE MEER*

12 eggs
3 cups boiling water
1 teaspoon anise seed
¼ cup soy sauce
5 tablespoons orange pekoe tea
1 tablespoon salt

Boil the eggs for 10 minutes so they should be hard. Take them out from the water and chill by putting them in cold water. Then you can take off from them the shells. Put in a pot the anise seed, soy sauce, tea and salt and pour over them from the kettle the 3 cups boiling water. Put in this the eggs and simmer nice for 1 hour. Now you can chill them and serve for a forshpeis. You'll have a surprise when you see the new color of the eggs.

*OY VAZE MEER: what you say when you realize you just buttered the bagel with a meat knife!

8

FISH BALLS TZATZ KELL LAH*

1 lb. flounder filet
10 water chestnuts
2 tablespoons cornstarch
2 tablespoons sherry
A couple pinches salt
1 nice egg
A pot hot oil

The fish chop up nice and fine (a blender is easier, if you have one); also the water chestnuts. This you'll mix together and also add the cornstarch, sherry, salt and the beaten up egg. When it's all mixed together already, you'll make from it little balls about ¾ or an inch big. Make hot the pot oil and fry the balls until they get a nice golden brown. Serve it with hot mustard and duck sauce.

TZATZ KELL LAH: what a Jewish child thinks is its first name.

EGG ROLL HAH DAH SAH*

FOR FLAT PANCAKES:

2 cups flour	A cup and a half water
A pinch salt	2 nice eggs

A pot full of fat so you can fry

First you should mix together everything but the fat until it's smooth. Take a small frying pan, about six inches, and put a little oil in it. Then you should pour some of the batter and let it spread over the whole pan. Watch out, it shouldn't get too hot. When it looks ready on one side, turn it over for a few seconds on the other. When that's done, put it on the side and make another. Do this a lot of times until you use up all the stuff.

NOW YOU'LL MAKE THE STUFFING:

A nice breast chicken cooked	2 tablespoons soy sauce
A couple pinches salt	1 little can mushrooms
A couple pinches sugar	1 cup bean sprouts
1 teaspoon cornstarch	A few chopped scallions
2 tablespoons oil or schmaltz	½ cup sliced onion

¼ cup bamboo shoots

10

The chicken should be cut into tiny pieces, but not too tiny. Mix it up with the salt, the sugar, the cornstarch and the soy sauce. Then let it stand. You'll come back in a minute.

Now take a tablespoon oil or schmaltz in a deep frying pan and put in the mushrooms, bean sprouts, scallions, onion and bamboo shoots. This you should sauté for a couple minutes. Then you'll put in the chicken and the stuff it's soaking in. Cook it for another couple minutes and let it cool.

When it's cooled enough, so you shouldn't get burned, you'll take a nice big tablespoon full and put it in the middle of one of the flat latkes you made before. Roll it like you are making a long thin package. To seal, brush with a beaten egg. Then do the rest.

Get the pot full of fat nice and hot (375°) and fry a few pieces at a time. You'll know that when it gets brown, you should take it out. Let it drain before you serve it.

On the table you should have some hot mustard, and some duck sauce. Also, a very good sauce for this is applesauce mixed with hot white horseradish. Chinese this sauce isn't, but it's good. This makes 8 to 10 delicious pieces.

* *HAH DAH SAH:* the Jewish answer to the D.A.R.

11

FOH NEE SHRIMP PUFFS*

One jar gefillte fish balls
One pot hot oil

Get the pot oil good and hot and put in the gefillte fish balls. Let them get a nice healthy brown and they're finished. Take them out from the oil, stick in them toothpicks and serve. Duck sauce and mustard is nice to dip in.

FOH NEE SHRIMP TOAST*

FOR THIS DELICACY, AGAIN YOU'LL NEED A POT HOT OIL. ALSO:

1 lb. flounder filet	A little salt
3 or 4 scallions	A little pepper
4 tablespoons soy sauce	Triangles of white bread

Take the fish, and chop it up, or put it in a blender. Mix in some chopped scallions, the soy sauce, salt and pepper. Shmear this on the pieces bread and cook it in the hot oil until it gets nice and brown. This is also good with duck sauce and mustard. It makes a nice forshpeis and a better heartburn. (Makes about 12 shtichlach).

* Not even from a *modern* Kosher Grandmother should you expect real shrimp!

12

STUFFED MUSHROOMS
MAH ZEL TUV*

20 nice large mushrooms
¾ lb. ground meat
3 tablespoons chopped scallions
3 tablespoons soy sauce
A few pinches salt
A little pinch pepper
1 tablespoon flour
1 cup beef or chicken broth

Wash the mushrooms nice and put away the stems for something else. Chop up together the meat and scallions they should be very fine. Now mix in a tablespoon soy sauce, salt, pepper and flour. Shape this into small balls and into the mushrooms you'll stuff. Now in a large frying pan you'll pour in the rest of the soy sauce and the broth. Put in the mushrooms with the stuffed side up, and put on the pan a cover, and for 20 minutes you should cook. If it's not done, don't worry, you'll cook a little more. This is a delicious forshpeis for Bar Mitzvahs, weddings, or Bris receptions.

* *MAH ZEL TUV:* what they told Columbus when he got back to Spain.

13

FRIED WON TON REB EH TSIN*

First comes the kreplach (also called won ton; also called ravioli—depending on your neighborhood).

FOR THE STUFFING YOU'LL TAKE:

A little schmaltz or oil 1 onion chopped
½ lb. chopped meat 2 pinches salt
A pinch pepper

Heat in the frying pan a little schmaltz or oil and put in the meat and onions. You'll cook for a few minutes until it's brown. Now put in the salt and pepper. Next, it should cool.

FOR THE DOUGH:

A cup and a half flour 2 tablespoons water
A pinch salt 1 fresh egg

Sift the flour together with the salt into a bowl. Then you'll blend in the egg and water. Put this on a table covered with a little flour and knead it smooth. Now cover it up and leave it for 10 minutes. Then with a rolling pin you'll roll it very thin. Cut it up into pieces 3 inches square. In each square, you'll put a little stuffing and fold it like a triangle. Squeeze the edges together and cook it in salted water for 15 minutes.

NOW YOU'LL TAKE:

2 tablespoons oil	1 teaspoon soy sauce
⅔ cup chopped onion	¾ cup beef or chicken broth
1 tablespoon cornstarch	A pot full of hot fat

Take the won ton and when the fat, it gets hot, put them in and fry on both sides. They should get brown. This should take about 10-15 minutes. Then put them on paper towels to drain off the oil. Take 2 tablespoons oil in a frying pan and cook in it the onions until tender and soft. While this cooks, mix together the cornstarch, soy sauce and broth. When the onions are ready pour in the mixture and mix up nice. Let it get good and thick and pour it over the fried won ton. This will serve about 4 people who, we'll make you a guarantee, will lick their fingers, especially if you forget to serve forks or chopsticks.

* *REB EH TSIN:* such a job for a nice Jewish girl!

HELZEL HONG KONG*

For this you should make a stuffing like for the EGG
ROLL HAH DAH SAH (see page 10). But only half as
much. Then take the neck skins from 3 or 4 chickens. (It
depends if they have long necks or short necks.) With a
needle and thread you should sew up one end of the neck,
push in the stuffing and sew up the other end. Do this until
you run out of necks or out of the stuffing. Next you should
make hot a pot oil and fry the helzel until it looks like two
weeks in Miami. Slice it in pieces and serve.

* HELZEL: the part of the chicken that if it gets wrung, it's not
Kosher.

16

SOUPS

BUB UH LUH WON
TON SOUP*

For this you'll make kreplach just like for the FRIED WON
TON REB EH TSIN (see page 14).

THEN YOU'LL MAKE THE SOUP:

4 cups nice chicken broth
½ cup cooked chicken shreds
½ cup celery chopped
A few pieces lettuce, watercress or spinach

Boil first the broth; then put in the chicken and the greens;
also the kreplach. Let it boil for another minute and you
can serve it even to a Mandarin, it's so good. Serves 4
Mandarins.

* *BUB UH LUH*: proposed name of the first Israeli atomic sub-
marine.

CHICKEN MUSHROOM
SOUP YID DIH SHA MAH MAH*

4 cups chicken broth	4 large mushrooms
1 small chopped onion	1 oz. egg noodles
1 teaspoon MSG	A few pieces lettuce, or water- cress

Put in the pot the broth and onion and MSG. Bring to a nice boil and throw in the sliced mushrooms and the egg noodles. Let it boil for another 10 minutes or so, put in then the pieces lettuce or watercress and serve. Serves 4 people. In China, it is known as Moo Goo Gai Tong; in Chinese restaurants, it is generally known as the one from Group A.

* *YID DIH SHA MAH MAH*: packs for her son, the astronaut, a thermos of hot chicken soup.

CUCUMBER SOUP GAY AH VEK*

> 4 cups nice chicken broth
> 10 sliced mushrooms
> 1 small can bamboo shoots
> ½ cup cooked chicken shreds
> 1 teaspoon soy sauce
> A pinch salt or two
> 1 teaspoon cornstarch
> 1 fat cucumber

Put in a pot the chicken broth, mushrooms, bamboo shoots, chicken shreds, soy sauce, salt and the cornstarch mixed in a little water. Then you'll light the fire and simmer for 20 minutes. While you're simmering, peel already the cucumber and cut it in pieces about ½ inch thick. When the soup has simmered for 20 minutes, put in the cucumber pieces and boil for 3 or 4 minutes. Serve it right away, it shouldn't get cold. 4 people this serves.

* *GAY AH VEK:* Mother, please! I'd rather do it myself!

FAR BLUN JED EGG DROP SOUP*

3 cups nice chicken broth
1 tablespoon soy sauce
A pinch salt or two
A teaspoon MSG
1 nice fresh egg
A little handful watercress
2 teaspoons cornstarch
2 tablespoons water

In a pot you'll heat the broth to a boil. Then add the soy sauce, salt and MSG. Make a thin mixture of the cornstarch with the water and add this to the soup and cook until it thickens slightly. Next you can beat the egg and add it to the soup very slowly; all the time you should mix. Take it off from the fire, add the watercress and serve.

* FAR BLUN JED is what a Jewish mother calls her son when he wants to join the Peace Corps instead of becoming a doctor.

EGG FLOWER SOUP PAY SAH DIK*

4 cups nice rich chicken broth
½ cup celery sliced
½ onion chopped
A few pinches salt
1 fresh egg
A handful lettuce, spinach, or watercress

In a pot, you should boil the broth. Next throw in the celery, onion and salt. When it boils again, you'll mix up the egg and stir it in. When you're through stirring, put in the lettuce or spinach in pieces and let it cook for a minute. It's a very nice soup for Pesach and it will serve 4 people.

* PAY SAH DIK: refers to the Jewish holiday when the carpets of America are blanketed with matzoh crumbs—from wall to wall.

LUCK SHEN SOUP*

¾ lb. egg noodles already cooked
1 tablespoon soy sauce
2 tablespoons schmaltz
A few pinches salt
1½ cups sliced chicken
1 cup mushrooms
½ cup bean sprouts
1 cup water chestnuts sliced
1 tablespoon cornstarch
½ cup water
4 cups chicken broth

Divide the noodles into serving bowls and put in each a little soy sauce. Melt the schmaltz in a frying pan, put in a little salt and brown the slices chicken. Then put in the mushrooms, bean sprouts and water chestnuts. Blend the cornstarch with a little water and also put in. Cover the pot and cook until the vegetables soften a bit and the sauce thickens. In another pot make hot the broth and pour on the noodles. Now you can put in each bowl some of the chicken and vegetable mixture. If your bowls are the same size as ours, you'll serve 4 people. If they are smaller, maybe you'll squeeze out for 6 people.

* LUCK SHEN is what the Italians, Jews and Chinese all claim to have invented—actually, it's Tahitian!

23

RICE, EGG & MATZOH DISHES

YUN TIF FRIED RICE*

2 tablespoons oil	A little chopped celery
1 big onion chopped	A little chopped green pepper
½ cup chopped leftover chicken	3 cups leftover rice
	2 fresh eggs
½ cup chopped leftover meat	1 tablespoon soy sauce

A few pinches salt (maybe)

Take a big frying pan, put in the oil it should get hot. Then fry the onion a little. Next, throw in the chicken, the meat and the vegetables. Then, you'll throw in the rice; give it once in a while a mix, until the whole thing gets a little brown Now you should make a little hole in the middle so the pan shows through. Stir up the eggs and pour them in the hole. When the eggs begin to fry a little, you should begin mixing up the whole thing. Also, pour in the spoon soy sauce and maybe a little salt if it needs. When it looks finished, it is. Serves maybe 5 or 6.

* YUN TIF: any holiday when you have to kiss all the relatives and Mom brings out the shnapps.

TUH MEL FRIED RICE WITH MUSHROOMS*

2 nice fresh eggs	4 cups cooked cold rice
3 tablespoons oil	2 teaspoons soy sauce
½ lb. mushrooms	A few pinches salt
1 medium onion chopped	A little pepper

Beat up the eggs and put in a frying pan a little oil. When the oil gets hot add the eggs and cook like a latke (pancake). This you'll cut into thin strips. Add in the pan a little more oil and throw in the onion, it should cook till it's tender. Then put in the rest of the oil and add the rice and the pieces egg. Mix together the soy sauce, salt, pepper and throw it also in. Cook over a medium fire until it all gets hot and serve right away. This is a good way to use up leftover rice. Serves 4 people.

* *TUH MEL*: the family reunion to celebrate when Grandma got her "citizen's papers."

VEGETABLE OMLET GIB AH KEEK*

1 nice onion
4 mushrooms
1 green pepper
3 sticks celery
3 tablespoons oil
5 fresh eggs
A few pinches salt
A little pinch pepper

Chop up the onion, make the mushrooms in slices and in pieces you'll cut the pepper. Also the celery you'll cut into tiny pieces. Now you can heat up a frying pan and put in the oil. When it gets hot you'll throw in the onions and let them get a golden brown. Then the other vegetables you can throw in and cook for about a minute. When it's done, from the pan you should take them out and drain. Now beat up the eggs and mix them in with the vegetables, salt and pepper. Put in a little more oil in the pan and fry nice the egg and vegetable mixture on a low fire until it's set. This you can cut up into pieces and serve.

* *GIB AH KEEK* means—look at the size of that diamond!

MATZOH BREI FOO YONG*

2 matzohs
1 medium onion sliced
3 tablespoons oil
4 spoons green pepper
   chopped

1-5 oz. can bamboo shoots
2 nice green scallions
¾ cup chopped pieces chicken,
   cooked
4 nice fresh eggs

First break up the matzoh into pieces and soak in water. While this is soaking, sauté the onion in a little oil until it's golden; then add the green pepper for a couple minutes. Now you can throw in also the bamboo shoots, chopped scallions and the chicken. Let cook for 2 more minutes. During this 2 minutes, you can drain the matzoh and add the eggs to it. Don't forget to mix nice. Now you can pour into the matzoh and egg mixture the vegetables and chicken. Mix this all together and fry with a little oil into latkes about the size of a tea saucer.

NOW FOR THE GRAVY:

1 cup water
1 tablespoon oil
1 teaspoon sugar
1 teaspoon salt
1 teaspoon soy sauce

1 teaspoon MSG
A pinch pepper
2 teaspoons cornstarch
together with 2 tablespoons
water

First you should boil the cup water and then add all the other things. Stir for half a minute and pour over each serving. This will make 2 people nice and full and it makes a good change from bagels and lox on Sunday morning.

* *MATZOH*: that new Jewish diet bread all the goyem are buying.

VEGETABLES

GREEN BEANS HOK MEE
NOH CHY NICK*

½ lb. nice steak
1 tablespoon soy sauce
1 teaspoon MSG
1 teaspoon sugar
1 teaspoon cornstarch

A few pinches salt
A pinch pepper
A little oil
1 package frozen green beans
½ cup water

The steak you'll cut up into small thin pieces (1" x 1" thin). In a bowl you'll put in the soy sauce, MSG, sugar, cornstarch, salt and pepper. Mix this up and put into it the steak, it should stand for a while (10 minutes). Heat the little oil in a frying pan and cook in it the steak for 5 minutes. While it's frying, you should stir. Then you can add the thawed beans, pour in the water and cook it for 15 minutes on a low fire. When it's finished it'll serve 4 people or 2 "nice & healthy" cousins who just dropped in.

* HOK MEE NOH CHY NICK: what Mom says when Irving tries to explain why he was kicked out of Hebrew School.

32

STRING BEANS TSUR RISS*

> 1 tablespoon oil
> 2 cloves garlic
> 1 medium onion
> 2 tablespoons soy sauce
> 1 lb. fresh string beans
> 1 cup chicken broth

Make hot a frying pan and put in the oil. Slice up the garlic and onion and fry for a while, it should get golden. Then you can add the soy sauce and the string beans, in pieces they should be broken. Pour in now the chicken broth and let the whole thing simmer for 8-10 minutes, or until they're tender, but not so soft there's no vitamins left. This should serve 4 people.

* *TSUR RISS:* when Tillie can't get a beauty parlor appointment in time for the Bar Mitzvah.

EGG PLANT GON IFF*

½ lb. eggplant
4 dried mushrooms soaked
A few slices bamboo shoots
3 or 4 slices nice cooked
chicken

A pot hot oil for deep-fry
1 tablespoon oil
Meat from 2 or 3 walnuts
A few almonds

SAUCE:

2 tablespoons soy sauce
2 tablespoons sherry
A pinch MSG

First you should peel the eggplant and cut it into wedges, about an inch big they should be. Then you'll cut these wedges into ½ inch pieces. Next the mushrooms, bamboo shoots and chicken you'll slice. Make nice and hot the pot oil and fry in it for 3 minutes the eggplant. Then you'll drain *very, very* well. In a frying pan, put a tablespoon oil and throw in the mushrooms, chicken and bamboo shoots and fry for a minute. Put in the eggplant and the sauce ingredients, and mix nice. Now you can put it on a plate so you can serve. Don't forget to put on top the nuts. This will serve two very hungry people. Sometimes it's nice to fix a little fancy dish even when you're not having company. Your husband will appreciate.

* *GON IFF:* the taxi driver that took you to your hotel in Los Angeles by way of San Diego.

34

CARROTS BUH BUH MY SUH*

5 or 6 nice carrots
1 tablespoon oil
1 cup water
2 tablespoons sugar
A few pinches salt
2 tablespoons vinegar
1 tablespoon cornstarch

Wash nice the carrots and in diagonal slices a half inch thick you'll cut them. Make hot a frying pan and put in the oil. When it's good and hot you'll sauté for a minute the carrots. Then throw in a half cup water. Now you'll cover and boil for 5 minutes until the carrots are soft enough so you can eat. Mix all together the sugar, salt, vinegar, cornstarch and the rest of the water. Put this in the pan with the carrots and let it cook for a little while, it should get thick. This makes a very nice side dish for 4 or 5 people—and it's full with vitamins. You should feed it to the children, it'll put roses in their cheeks.

* *BUH BUH MY SUH* is the ridiculous story that carrots will put roses in your cheeks.

35

SPINACH MISH AH GAHS*

1 lb. fresh spinach
2 tablespoons oil
A few pinches salt
¼ cup chicken broth
1 small can bamboo shoots
8 nice mushrooms

Wash good the spinach, it shouldn't be sandy, and cut it up in 2 inch pieces. Make hot a frying pan and add the oil. When it's good and hot, throw in the salt and the spinach and for two minutes you should fry. Then you can pour in the broth and throw in the bamboo shoots and mushrooms. This you'll cook for a few more minutes and serve right away, it shouldn't get cold.

* MISH AH GAHS: soliciting for the U.J.A. at the Egyptian Embassy.

MIXED VEGETABLES HAH ZAH RYE*

12 shelled almonds
12 chestnuts
 4 tablespoons oil
 ½ cup diced celery
 6 nice mushrooms
12 water chestnuts in small
     chunks
 1 cup bean sprouts

 1 small can bamboo shoots,
     sliced
 1 cup lettuce
 ¼ cup soy sauce
 A pinch or two salt
 2 tablespoons sherry
 1 teaspoon cornstarch
 3 cups nice fresh chicken
     broth

In a pot hot water the almonds and chestnuts (*not* the water chestnuts) you should boil for 10 minutes. Then you can take them out from the water and the chestnuts you'll peel. Make hot a large frying pan and put in the oil. Then you should throw in the celery, mushrooms sliced, the water chestnuts, bean sprouts, bamboo shoots, almonds and chestnuts. Let this cook for 5 minutes making sure you stir. Then add in the lettuce, soy sauce, salt, sherry, cornstarch, and chicken broth. Cover the pan and cook on a low fire until all the vegetables are done. Be careful it doesn't cook too much, it shouldn't be mushy. Serve nice and hot with rice.

* *HAH ZAH RYE:* the meat that was taken out from this recipe so it should be Kosher.

FISH

FAH SHTUNK KEN AH FISH ROLL*

3 nice fresh eggs	1 tablespoon chopped scallions
1 tablespoon water	2 tablespoons chopped water
2 tablespoons oil	chestnuts
¾ cup chopped flounder (for	A little pinch salt
this is good a blender)	1 tablespoon soy sauce

Put the tablespoon water in the eggs and beat them up. Then make hot a little of the oil in a large frying pan and pour half the eggs in the pan so it covers all over and is thin. Fry it until it's nice and set and then turn it over so you'll cook the other side. Put it aside so it'll cook and fry the rest of the egg mixture the same way. Now you'll mix together the chopped fish, scallions, water chestnuts, salt and soy sauce. Put half of it on one of the egg pieces and smooth it out nice, it should cover all over. Then you can roll it up like a piece strudel, put some flour on the edges and press the edges together so they don't come apart. Do the same thing with the other piece egg. Cut the rolls up with a sharp knife (you shouldn't cut yourself) in ¼ inch slices. Make hot in the frying pan the rest of the oil and fry the slices so they'll be a nice golden brown. This makes enough for 6 people.

SAUCE:

1½ tablespoons soy sauce	1 tablespoon cornstarch
¾ cup water	½ teaspoon sugar

Mix together the soy sauce and cornstarch so it should be smooth. Add the water and sugar and for 5 minutes you'll boil. Pour on the slices and serve.

* *FAH SHTUNK KEN AH:* even his best friends won't tell him!

40

HADDOCK YEN TAH*

6 mushrooms
1 lb. haddock filet
1 tablespoon cornstarch
2 tablespoons oil
1 fat clove garlic minced
2 nice scallions
½ can bamboo shoots
1 tablespoon vinegar
4 tablespoons sherry
A few pinches salt

First you'll take the mushrooms and cut them in chunks. Now, the fish you'll cut into pieces about an inch or two square and sprinkle on the cornstarch all over. Then in a frying pan you'll heat the oil and put in the garlic and fry for a minute. Next put in the fish and sauté for 2 or 3 minutes more. Take out the fish from the pan and put aside for a while. Add to the pan the scallions chopped, the bamboo shoots, the mushrooms, the vinegar, sherry and salt. Cook this for a couple minutes, you shouldn't forget to stir. Now you can add a half teaspoon cornstarch mixed in with a little water and then the fish and cook for about 2 or 3 minutes. If your neighbor comes to your door to ask what smells, invite the Yen Tah in for dinner.

* *YEN TAH*: a free-lance social worker.

FISH NEH BISH*

1½ lbs. filet of sole	2 tablespoons oil
2 scallions	2 nice fresh eggs
2 tablespoons soy sauce	2 teaspoons cornstarch
1 tablespoon sherry	A pinch sugar
A few pinches salt	3 tablespoons water
1 small can pineapple chunks	

First you'll take a knife and cut up each piece fish across in strips an inch wide. Then chop up the scallions and with the soy sauce, sherry and salt, you'll mix. Put in this the pieces fish and soak for a few minutes. Now you'll heat up the oil in a frying pan. While it heats, beat up the eggs and mix in the cornstarch. In this, the fish you'll dip. Then you can fry the pieces fish for a couple minutes on each side so it's cooked. When it's ready, you'll drain and put on a serving dish. Next the sugar and water you'll add to the leftover dipping mixture, also the pineapple chunks. Put this into the pan and cook for a few minutes until it gets thick and almost clear looking. Now you can pour it on the fish and it's ready to serve about 4 people.

* NEH BISH: a man who asks the Chinese waiter if he can substitute french frys for rice.

HALIBUT CANTONESE
LANTZ MAHN*

1½ lbs. halibut in small
 chunks
1 tablespoon oil
2 mashed cloves garlic

1 chopped onion
1 sliced scallion
1 tablespoon chopped celery
1 nice fresh egg

Put the halibut in a pot water and boil for 2 minutes. Then you can put in a frying pan the oil and brown the onions. When they're nice and brown, put in the chunks fish.

SAUCE:

1½ cups water
1 tablespoon oil
A few pinches salt
3 teaspoons soy sauce

1 teaspoon MSG
A pinch pepper
2 tablespoons cornstarch in 3
 tablespoons water

Mix together the stuff for the sauce, but not the cornstarch. Pour this on the fish together with the garlic, scallions and celery. Put on the pan a cover and you'll simmer for 2 minutes. Now beat up nice the egg and pour slow into the sauce. Keep mixing while you pour. After this, you should pour in the cornstarch mixture and stir it up good. Let this whole thing cook until it gets thick.

* *CANTONESE LANTZ MAHN*: that's funny; you don't *look* Jewish!

HALIBUT SHREDS GON TZE MAH KER*

2 tablespoons oil	¼ cup soy sauce
1 lb. flaked halibut	¼ cup sherry
¼ teaspoon ginger powder	A few pinches sugar

4 nice scallions sliced

Heat up in the frying pan a little oil and fry the fish flakes and ginger for a couple minutes. Then throw in the soy sauce, sherry, sugar and the sliced scallions. Let this cook on a low fire and don't forget to stir. This will be ready when most of the juice disappears. 4 nice servings this should make.

* GON TZE MAH KER: the Uncle Sol in everyone's family, who says don't do anything 'til you call me first.

FISH CAKE SHA LOM*

1½ lbs. flounder filet	1 tablespoon soy sauce
1 cup blanched almonds	1 tablespoon cornstarch
A few pinches salt	in a little water
2 sliced scallions	¾ cup oil

Chop up nice the fish (in a blender it's easier) and the almonds. Then you can mix in the scallions, salt, soy sauce, cornstarch mixture and 1½ tablespoons oil. This you can pat into nice flat latkes, about 2 tablespoons to a latke. Make hot the rest of the oil in the frying pan and fry for a few minutes until they get brown on both sides. This will make enough for 5 or 6 people, they should live and be well.

* SHA LOM: Stanley's first word to Dr. Livingston.

44

FISH BAH LAH BOO STAH*

1 nice 2 lb. carp
¼ cup oil
½ teaspoon powdered ginger
3 nice sliced scallions
3 cloves garlic chopped
A few pinches salt
½ cup sliced mushrooms
1 tablespoon sherry
3 tablespoons soy sauce
1 cup vegetable stock
A pinch sugar
½ teaspoon anise seed

Leave whole the fish but clean it nice and then dry it. Next you can make a few cuts with a knife on each side. Put in the oil in a frying pan and get it good and hot. Fry the fish for a little while, it should get nice and brown. On both sides you shouldn't forget to do this. Then pour off some of the oil and add the ginger, scallions, garlic, salt, mushrooms, sherry, soy sauce, stock, sugar and anise seed. Cover the pan and cook on a low fire for 30 minutes. Maybe you should also turn the fish once in a while so it should cook nice. This will serve 4 people, if you serve also a few other things.

* BAH LAH BOO STAH: someone who cleans her house before the maid comes, she shouldn't find it dirty.

TUNA LUCK SHEN
GRO SING GUHS*

2 tablespoons oil
1 sliced onion
1 cup bean sprouts
1 small can bamboo shoots
1 can mushrooms
A little green pepper chopped

A little chopped celery
1 cup vegetable stock
¼ cup soy sauce
2 cans tuna fish (7 oz. each)
A box thin noodles (12 oz.)
1 tablespoon cornstarch
4 tablespoons water

Heat the oil in a frying pan and cook in it the onions for a few minutes. Then you'll put in all the vegetables, stock, soy sauce and the tuna fish. This you should cover and cook maybe 12 minutes.

While this is on the stove, you'll cook the noodles like the box says.

After the tuna mish-mash has cooked for 12 minutes, mix the cornstarch with the water and pour it in. In a minute the whole thing will get a little thick. Then it's ready to mix with the noodles. This should be for 6 people, they should live and be well.

* GRO SING GUHS: the East Coast matrimonial bureau for teen-age spinsters.

FOWL

PINEAPPLE CHICKEN FAY
GEL LAH*

2 nice egg yolks	1 pot hot oil
⅔ cup water	1 teaspoon cornstarch
3 tablespoons flour	¼ cup nice chicken broth
A pinch salt	½ teaspoon powdered ginger
1 teaspoon soy sauce	½ cup pineapple juice
1½ cups cooked chicken in bite–size pieces	1 cup chunks canned pineapple

Mix together nice the egg yolks, water, flour, salt and half the soy sauce. Now you'll dip in the pieces chicken and fry it in the oil until it's good and brown. Next mix together the cornstarch, chicken broth, ginger, the rest of the soy sauce and the pineapple juice. Put this in a pot and you'll boil until it gets thick. Put in the pineapple chunks, and on the chicken pieces you'll pour. Serve it nice and hot with rice, for 6 people. This dish, believe me, they'll love on Fire Island.

* FAY GEL LAH: "my son, the dancer."

48

CHICKEN GAH BAR DEEN*

4 lbs. nice roasting chicken
¼ cup soy sauce
3 tablespoons sherry
A few pinches salt
A little pinch pepper
½ teaspoon powdered ginger

2 chopped cloves garlic
8 dried mushrooms
2 tablespoons oil
1 cup nice chicken broth
1½ tablespoons cornstarch
A pinch sugar

Wash and dry nice the chicken and mix together 3 tablespoons soy sauce, salt, sherry, pepper, ginger and garlic. Rub good into the chicken and soak for an hour. Now soak the mushrooms for 30 minutes and then cut into nice slices. Next make hot the oil in a casserole and brown in it the chicken. Now you can throw in the mushrooms and ¾ of the broth and cook on a low fire for a half hour, it should be tender. When it's done, take out from the pot the chicken and you'll chop yourself up in little bite-size pieces. Next you'll mix the cornstarch with the rest of the broth and the rest of the soy sauce and the sugar. Put this in the casserole with the juice that's there already and keep stirring it until it boils and gets good and thick. Now you can throw in the pieces chicken and cook for a little while longer until it's all hot. This will serve 4 "piece goods" salesmen.

* GAH BAR DEEN: what Bar Mitzvah suits used to be made of.

VELVET CHICKEN MEH GILL LAH*

8 ounces of chicken breast
1 cup nice chicken broth
2 teaspoons salt
2 teaspoons sherry

3 teaspoons cornstarch mixed
in a little water
8 egg whites
A pot oil so you can deep fry

1 teaspoon MSG

Remove the meat from the bone and mince it up nice and fine. (This is very important; make sure it should be a creamy paste. A blender for this is perfect.) Add to this 6 tablespoons of the chicken broth and mix it up good. Then you should add the salt, sherry and half the cornstarch mixture to the egg whites and with the chicken mix it. Now in a pot of good hot oil, you'll pour in some of the mixture and let it cook for 10-15 seconds. Then stir the oil a little underneath (be careful you shouldn't touch the chicken) so you'll help it rise to the top. When it finally rises, you can turn it over so the other side should also cook. When it gets a nice golden brown take it out from the oil and start all over until all the stuff is used up. Put them on paper, they should drain; and then put in a dish so you can serve. Next take the rest of the broth, cornstarch and MSG and heat it up. When it gets good and thick, pour it over the chicken and serve. This should be enough for 4 people and maybe one of them will be able to give you an idea on how to use up 8 leftover egg yolks.

* *MEH GILL LAH*: a Jewish Federal case.

CELESTIAL CHICKEN IN
SILVER PACKAGE OH
REE YEN TAH*

2 nice chicken breasts	4 tablespoons chopped scallions
3 tablespoons soy sauce	
1 tablespoon oil	1 tablespoon chopped water chestnuts
½ cup mushrooms chopped	
A pinch ginger	1 tablespoon sherry

A pot hot oil so you can fry

Take from the breasts chicken, the skin and bones. With a mallet, pound flat the pieces chicken and cut into 2 inch squares. Sprinkle on a little soy sauce and let stand for a few minutes. While it's standing, heat a little oil in a pan and sauté the vegetables for a few minutes. Then pour in the rest of the soy sauce, ginger and sherry. Let it cool and then spread a little bit on each piece chicken. Fold over the chicken squares (like little envelopes they should be) and wrap also like an envelope in a piece aluminum foil (3 or 4 inches square). When they are all made and wrapped, let them cool for a while and then deep fry them for about 4 minutes in the hot oil (375°). Makes 10-12 pieces. When the neighbors smell this cooking, they'll think you've gone "trafe"—but you shouldn't worry. The Rabbi says it's Kosher, so who cares from the neighbors?

* OH REE YEN TAH: a lady Chinese gossip.

CHICKEN GOY YIM*

1 lb. chicken breasts   1 scallion
3 cups boiling water   ½ teaspoon pepper

SAUCE:

2 tablespoons sherry   1 teaspoon sugar
2 tablespoons oil   ¼ teaspoon vinegar
5 tablespoons soy sauce

Cover the chicken with hot boiling water and for 10-12 minutes it should cook. While it's cooking you can mix up the sauce and heat. Chop up in pieces the scallion. When the chicken finishes cooking you'll take a cleaver (watch out you shouldn't cut the fingers) and cut the breasts crosswise right through the bone in pieces ¾ of an inch wide. This you can put on a serving dish, sprinkle on the chopped scallions and pepper. Also, the sauce you shouldn't forget to pour on. This will serve 2 people, but also make lots of tea. For salt-free diets, this isn't.

* GOY YIM: what some of our best friends are.

CHICKEN PIPP ICK*

2 tablespoons oil
3 lb. fryer chopped in pieces, bite–size
2 cups chopped water chestnuts
2 cups chopped mushrooms
1 large onion sliced

4 stalks celery in thin pieces
2 nice handfuls spinach
4 scallions
2 cups bamboo shoots
A tiny pinch ginger
1 cup nice chicken broth

SAUCE:

2 tablespoons cornstarch
3 teaspoons soy sauce
A pinch salt

A little pinch pepper
A little pinch sugar
A pinch MSG

4 tablespoons water

Make hot the oil in a pot and brown in it the chicken. Then add all the vegetables, the ginger and the broth and simmer for twenty minutes. Next blend the sauce ingredients together and add to the mixture and stir until it gets nice and thick. This serves about 5 people, they should live to be a hundred and twenty.

* PIPP ICK: the first part of his anatomy a baby discovers.

CHICKEN WALNUT AH MENCH*

1 medium size chicken	½ cup chopped celery
3 tablespoons soy sauce	6 water chestnuts sliced
2 tablespoons sherry	½ cup bamboo shoots
1 tablespoon cornstarch	1 medium onion sliced
1 cup walnuts shelled	½ cup bean sprouts
6 tablespoons oil	A pinch salt
½ cup sliced mushrooms	¼ cup nice chicken broth

Take from the chicken all the meat and cut into ½ inch pieces. Mix together the soy sauce, sherry, and cornstarch and soak in it the meat. Blanch the walnuts and fry in 2 tablespoons oil so they get brown. Then you should drain. Now you'll take a hot frying pan and put in 2 tablespoons oil. In this you'll put all the vegetables and salt and sauté until they are about half done. Now you'll take out and put aside. Put 2 more tablespoons oil in the pan and put in the pieces chicken. This you'll fry for a few minutes until it's cooked. When it's ready, you'll put back the vegetables and on this pour in the broth and put in the walnuts. Heat for another 2 minutes and it's ready to serve.

* *AH MENCH:* Uncle Leon, the lawyer; he has his own office.

CHICKEN LUCK SHEN DAH REE ANN*

¼ lb. nice, rich egg noodles
1 tablespoon oil
A pinch salt
1 cup sliced Chinese celery cabbage, (or American celery)
½ cup bean sprouts

A few nice mushrooms
¼ lb. cooked, diced chicken
¼ cup water
1 tablespoon soy sauce
1 teaspoon MSG
A pinch sugar
A little pepper

In a pot with 2 quarts boiling water you should cook the noodles for 8 minutes and then drain. Next heat a frying pan with a little oil on a high fire. Add the salt, celery cabbage, bean sprouts, mushrooms and chicken. Keep mixing while you fry it for 2 or 3 minutes. After this, pour in the water and the noodles, they should be on top. Cover the pan and cook for about 2 to 3 minutes. Now you can mix in the soy sauce, MSG, sugar and pepper. Cook for another minute and you're all done. It's a very good way to use up the leftovers from Friday night's boiled chicken.

* DAH REE ANN: proposed site of the first Jewish sit-in.

TURKEY CHOW MEIN HUTZ PAH*

2 tablespoons oil
2 nice onions sliced
2 cups sliced celery
¾ lb. sliced mushrooms
1½ cups nice chicken broth
1 small can water chestnuts
1 cup bean sprouts

1 small can bamboo shoots
3 tablespoons soy sauce
1 tablespoon cornstarch
3 cups shredded cooked turkey
A package crisp Chinese noodles

Make hot in a frying pan the oil and fry the onions until they get tender. Then add the celery, mushrooms and broth and for 5 minutes you'll cook. Throw in the water chestnuts, bean sprouts and bamboo shoots and cook for a few minutes more. Now mix together the soy sauce and the cornstarch and throw also into the pan. Keep on cooking and stirring until it gets nice and thick. Now you can put in the turkey and cook for a few minutes more, it should get hot. When it's all ready, you'll pour it on the noodles and serve right away, it mustn't get cold. Believe me, this is the best way to finish up from Thanksgiving.

* HUTZ PAH: describes anyone who asks a bus driver, at the rush hour, if he has change of $5.

ROAST DUCK FAH BRENT*

A nice 5 lb. duck
4 teaspoons honey
¼ cup chicken broth
4 teaspoons sugar
1 tablespoon soy sauce
A pinch salt

Mix together everything but the duck. In this mixture you'll soak for an hour the duck. Then on a rack in a roasting pan with a little water in the bottom, put the bird. Place this in a 350° oven for 2 hours. Every once in a while you should baste a little. For the last 10 minutes, turn up the oven to high so the duck gets nice and crisp and brown. When it's all done, cut the duck into pieces and serve with duck sauce. About 4 people should make a meal from this.

If you're among friends, serve toothpicks after this. (The pretty colored ones are nice for a festive touch.)

FAH BRENT: what happens to the food in the oven when the timer breaks down and Mom's been on the phone who knows how long!

ROAST DUCK QVEH CHING*

A nice 5 lb. duck
1 cup soy sauce
2 tablespoons   powdered   ginger
A little oil

Clean good the duck and take out as much fat as you can.
Then mix together in a pot the soy sauce, ginger, the duck
and enough water so you'll cover. Now you'll boil for an
hour on a low flame. When it's ready, take out the duck and
throw away the liquid. With a little oil you should brush
the duck all over and put it on a rack in a roasting pan.
Roast it in the oven at 425° for 45 minutes until the duck
is tender. Then you'll turn up the oven to high for 5
minutes so the skin should get nice and crisp. This should
serve 4 people.

* *QVEH CHING:* when you ask someone how he feels and he
tells you.

VUS MAHKS DOO DUCKLING*

1-4 lb. duckling
2 tablespoons oil
A pinch salt
A pinch pepper
1 small can pineapple chunks

1 green pepper in pieces
A few chopped scallions
2 tablespoons cornstarch
2 teaspoons soy sauce
¼ cup water

In boiling water cover the duck and cook for 45 minutes, it should be tender. Take out the duck and save the broth. (If you let it boil by itself for a while it'll be richer.) Put in a large frying pan the oil, salt and pepper and get it hot. In the meanwhile, you can cut the duck into serving pieces and when the oil is hot you'll fry for a while, it should get brown all over. Then you'll add 1½ cups of the duck broth skimmed, the pineapple chunks and the green pepper. For 10 minutes this should cook. Near the end you can throw in the scallions. While it's still cooking at the end of the 10 minutes, you'll mix together the cornstarch, soy sauce and water and this you'll also throw in. Let it cook for a few minutes more so it thickens and it's nice and hot. Serve it right away with rice. It's enough for 4 people, and a nice change from Friday night boiled chicken.

* *VUS MAHKS DOO?* the first telegraph message ever sent.

You should bite your tongue!

PORK

MEAT

BEEF FLON KEN SWEET
AND SOUR*

½ lb. nice lean beef   1 teaspoon cornstarch
2 tablespoons soy sauce   3 tablespoons oil
             8 or 10 radishes

SAUCE:

1 tablespoon cornstarch
⅓ cup vinegar   ⅓cup sugar

First you'll slice very thin the beef and you'll mix together the soy sauce and cornstarch. Smear all over the beef slices with this mixture. In a frying pan, you'll put 2 tablespoons oil and begin to heat it. When it's hot, it's time to put in the vinegar, sugar and cornstarch, you shouldn't forget to mix. Then you can throw in the beef slices and let them cook until they get just a teeny bit brown. When that happens, you can add the radishes sliced and cook just long enough so they get hot. If you cook longer, they won't be crisp; they'll be, as said in Chinese, "Vee ah shmah tah." Serve it right away with other dishes so no one should get hungry. We can't tell you how many persons this serves unless we know what else you're serving with it.

* FLON KEN: you were expecting maybe porterhouse?

64

BEEF SHIK SUH WITH CAULIFLOWER*

¾ lb. lean beef	1 small head cauliflower
2 tablespoons oil	1 lb. shelled peas
1 small onion chopped	½ cup bean sprouts
2 cloves garlic minced	½ cup mushrooms
1 cup beef broth	½ cup bamboo shoots

A few pinches salt

SAUCE:

2 tablespoons cornstarch	½ cup water
3 teaspoons soy sauce	2 teaspoons sherry

Slice thin the beef. Into the frying pan put the oil and get it good and hot; then add the beef, garlic, onion and cook until the meat gets nice and brown. Then pour in the beef broth and the cauliflower broken into 'flowerlets' and the rest of the vegetables and the salt. Cover it up; make a low fire and cook for about 15 minutes. While it's cooking, mix together the cornstarch, soy sauce, water and sherry. Then after the 15 minutes, pour this mixture in and cook until it gets thick. Serves about 3 or 4 people. If the grandchildren are coming for dinner, have chopsticks at the table at least. But have plenty napkins also.

* *SHIK SUH:* what Liz Taylor used to be.

BLUSHING BEEF SHLUH MEEL*

½ lb. steak | A few pinches salt
A little oil | 4 tablespoons water
4 tomatoes | 1 teaspoon soy sauce
1 tablespoon cornstarch | A pinch or two sugar

Slice the meat into very thin slices almost like paper. Then make hot the oil and fry the meat very quickly. Take out from the pan the meat, skin the tomatoes and put them in to warm up a little. While it's warming, you can mix together the cornstarch, salt, water, soy sauce and sugar. Then put the meat back with the tomatoes and add the mixture. Heat it until it's thick. It should serve from 4 to 5 people, if you are also serving other things, and maybe you should.

* SHLUH MEEL: he asks an Egyptian diplomat to speak at a Bonds for Israel rally.

MEAT THREADS KUPP DRAY NISH WITH VEGETABLES*

2 teaspoons oil
2 medium onions chopped
1½ cups chicken broth
2 tablespoons soy sauce
1 lb. steak cut into *thin* strips
1 cup sliced mushrooms
1 cup bamboo shoots

1 cup sliced water chestnuts
1 cup bean sprouts
5 leaves Chinese celery (or American celery)
4 scallions chopped
1 teaspoon sugar
A few pieces watercress

1 teaspoon MSG

Heat very hot the oil and sauté the onions. Then add some of the broth and soy sauce and stir for a few minutes. Add the rest of the ingredients except the MSG and cook for 15 minutes. Turn off the heat and add the MSG. Mix it up good and serve it with rice or some nice kasha. Serves 3. This you make a mistake if you don't serve with *fleischadik* chopsticks.

* *KUPP DRAY NISH:* this you have when the wedding is cancelled after the gifts have started arriving.

67

BEEF FON DOO*

For this you'll need a half pound steak each. Then you should cut up the steak into pieces just big enough for a good bite.

On the table you'll put a chafing dish with a pot full of hot oil.

Everybody should have a long fork. Stick it into the piece meat and put into the hot oil. Leave it for a minute or so and when it comes out . . . oh boy!

Then you can dip it into duck sauce and hot mustard or even the applesauce with horseradish. This is so exotic you shouldn't know from it.

(So your guests shouldn't go hungry, be sure to serve other things with this, like maybe vegetables, rice . . . the usual . . . but try candlelight . . . that, with the flame from the chafing dish . . . such ooh's and aah's you'll get from the family!)

---

* FON DOO: this is not a Jewish word . . . it's Swiss. But it's all right, you shouldn't worry . . . with the Swiss we never had any tsurris.

SAH DRAY TAH BEEF*

2 tablespoons oil
A pinch or two salt
A pinch pepper
1 lb. nice steak sliced thin
2 diced up onions
2 cloves garlic

1 cup chicken or beef broth
A few mushrooms sliced
2 green peppers diced
4 red tomatoes small, chunks
2 tablespoons cornstarch
2 teaspoons soy sauce

¼ cup water

In a hot frying pan you'll put the oil and salt and pepper. In this you should fry the slices steak together with the onion and garlic. When it gets brown the steak, you can add already the cup of broth and the diced green peppers and mushrooms. This you'll cook for about 10 minutes with the cover on. Then you'll throw in the tomato chunks and cook for another minute. While it's cooking, you'll hurry up and mix together the cornstarch, soy sauce and water. Throw this in the pan and cook until it gets thick and the whole thing is good and hot. This you should serve with boiled rice. It's enough for 4 people.

* *SAH DRAY TAH:* a baseball player who wants to play in the Arab League.

BEEF GOY ISH AH KUPP*

1 lb. nice steak	¼ teaspoon ginger
3 tablespoons oil	2 tablespoons soy sauce
2 big onions	1 teaspoon MSG
3 cloves garlic	A pinch or two salt
1 lb. mushrooms	A little pepper
1 cup chicken broth	3 teaspoons cornstarch

First you should cut the steak into very thin slices about ⅛ inch thick and about 2 inches long. (Exact you don't have to be, nobody will measure.) Then put 2 tablespoons oil into a frying pan and make it good and hot. Into this put the steak slices and fry it until it gets brown. You'll also find a little juice in the pan after this, so take out from the pan the steak and the juice, and put on the side for a while. Then put the other spoon oil into the pan and fry the onions, you shouldn't forget to slice, and the garlic. When this is soft and golden you can throw in the sliced mushrooms and cook for a little while more. Then you should put back the steak slices and juice, and put in the chicken broth, ginger, soy sauce, MSG, salt and pepper. Let this cook for about 3 minutes. Add the cornstarch, first mixed with a little water and cook 2 minutes more. Serve with rice to about 3 or 4 people.

* *GOY ISH AH KUPP:* refers to anyone who pays a retail price when he can get it wholesale.

SWEET AND PUNGENT BEEF
CHUNKS OY GAH VALT*

1½ lbs. steak	¾ cup white vinegar
2 fresh eggs	A few pinches salt
1 crushed garlic clove	½ cup sugar
¾ cup cornstarch	2 cups water
A pot hot oil	2 green peppers cut into
1 No. 2 can chunks	pieces
pineapple	2 nice tomatoes in pieces

The steak you'll cut into one inch pieces. Then beat up the eggs and the piece garlic together and dip in the beef. Then, in a half cup cornstarch you'll roll around the beef, and then put them into the hot oil and cook until it's brown. Then you'll put them on paper, they should drain. Take from the can pineapple the juice, and mix it with the rest of the cornstarch. Then mix in the vinegar, salt, sugar and water. Cook this on a low fire for a few minutes until it's nice and thick. Then throw in the pineapple, the green peppers, the tomatoes and the beef chunks. Keep cooking for about 5 minutes and it's ready to serve about 6 people. (This even the daughter-in-law will really enjoy.)

* *OY GAH VALT:* what you say on Yuntif in synagogue when the lady in front of you is wearing the same hat you are!

PEPPER STEAK SHAY
NUH KIN DUH*

4 tablespoons oil	1 clove minced garlic
1 lb. steak in little pieces	1 chopped scallion
A pinch pepper	1 cup chicken broth
A few pinches salt	1 tablespoon soy sauce
3 nice size peppers	4 tablespoons water

2 tablespoons cornstarch

First you should brown the meat in a little oil and then sprinkle on the salt and pepper. Then you can add the peppers, garlic and scallion. On this, pour the chicken broth and cover and cook for ten minutes. Now you can mix together the soy sauce; water and cornstarch also add. Cook for a few more minutes until it gets thick and it's ready to serve about 4 people. It's also nice to put a little rice on the table, or maybe even some noodles. If those stubborn kids couldn't make it for dinner, you should freeze the leftovers. Or better yet, it won't kill you to eat it for 2 days.

* SHAY NUH KIN DUH: those kids from next door who put their feet on the new sofa.

CUCUMBER VEAL MEES KITE*

½ lb. veal
2 teaspoons cornstarch
A pinch salt
2 teaspoons water

1 tablespoon oil
4 nice mushrooms sliced
1 nice peeled cucumber in
small chunks

3 teaspoons soy sauce

First, cut up the veal in nice little strips. Then you can mix together the cornstarch, salt, and water, and cover the pieces veal with this paste. Make hot the oil in a frying pan and throw in the slices mushroom and the cucumber. For 3 minutes you should cook, and don't forget to stir. Then you can put in the strips veal and cook for another 7 or 8 minutes. Pour on the soy sauce, mix it in nice, and cook for 2 minutes. Now you're done and you can serve. Make more if you're fixing for more than 2 people . . . Such a flavor!

* MEES KITE: what they called her before the "nose job."

BARBEQUED RIBS TZEL TZUH*

2 lbs. lamb ribs cut into strips   2 teaspoons white vinegar
3 tablespoons honey   3 tablespoons duck sauce
¼ cup soy sauce   2 tablespoons oil
¼ cup ginger ale

The ribs should be cut up into not too big pieces, so with your fingers you can eat. Then you'll mix all together the other things and let the ribs marinate in them for an hour or so. After that, you'll put on a rack the ribs and put them in the oven (350°) for an hour and a quarter. You shouldn't forget to baste every once in a while. Remember, the more you baste, the better they taste. When the oven time is up put the ribs under the broiler for a minute or two, they should get nice and brown. You can serve with a little duck sauce 4 people.

* *TZEL TZUH*: the Jewish ginger ale Mr. Lipschitz delivers every Friday.

DESSERT

GOLDEN CUSTARD ZEI
GUH ZINT*

3 fresh egg yolks
½ cup flour
2 tablespoons sugar
A little cornstarch
A pinch salt

1 cup milk
1 teaspoon almond extract
A pot hot oil
2 more tablespoons sugar
2 tablespoons grated almonds

Beat nice the egg yolks so they'll get thick. Then you'll sift together the flour with the sugar, salt and 1 tablespoon cornstarch. Pour a little of this into the egg yolks, then pour also a little milk, then a little more of the flour mixture. Keep pouring and mixing a little of each until it's all used up. Put this whole mish-mash in a double boiler and cook until it gets thick, you shouldn't forget to stir. When it's thick put in the almond extract . . . and mix. Now you'll smear a little butter all over a flat pan and the mixture you'll pour in. Cover it nice and put it in the refrigerator so it should get cold. Then you can cut into small squares and roll around in the cornstarch. Put it next into the pot hot oil and deep fry it until it gets a nice brown color. Take it out from the oil and drain thoroughly. Then mix together the sugar and almonds and roll around in it, it should cover all over. This makes enough for 4 people on high calorie diets.

(Of course you know it's not Kosher to serve this right after a meat dish. But you can serve it first . . . or 6 hrs. after a meat meal . . . but that would mean a *very* early dinner. So better you should save this dish for a fish night.)

* *ZEI GUH ZINT*: Lucrezia Borgia's favorite toast.

BANANAS MEH SHU GAH*

2 medium size bananas, sliced in chunks
6 tablespoons sugar
2 tablespoons oil

Heat in the pan a little oil and fry for 5 minutes the pieces banana. While you're frying you can heat the sugar in a pot until it melts. When the bananas are fried, into the melted sugar you should put them . . . and make sure they are all over covered. Serve them already before the sugar hardens.

On the table, in front of each person, there should be a dish cold water. Each person picks up a piece banana and dips it into the water. This makes it cool so your mouth you shouldn't burn. Be careful you don't serve this too much. From all that sugar, the teeth could fall out.

Serves 2 good customers for my son, the dentist.

* *MEH SHU GAH* refers to people who write Chinese-Kosher Cookbooks.

CANDIED DATES ZOFF TIKK*

½ lb. large pitted dates   1 cup sugar
¾ cup cold water   ⅛ teaspoon cream of tartar

First you should take each date and stick in a toothpick. Then mix together the sugar, cream of tartar and the water and cook until it's syrupy. You will know this when it's dropped from the spoon a little it makes a thread. Then take off from the fire and dip in each date so it should be all covered. Then you can let it cool and harden. You can also substitute for the dates, some pineapple, dried apricots, pieces banana or a mixture of all. After a dessert like this, be sure to brush well the teeth.

* ZOFF TIKK: a girl who is "nice & healthy" and will never wear a size 8.

 ## LYCHEE FRUIT SALAD
SHMUH GEH GHEE*

1 cup canned lychee
1 can fruit salad *or* 2 cups fresh mixed orange pieces,
   grapes, pineapple pieces, bananas, etc.

Mix together and serve chilled with maybe a little shredded coconut sprinkled on.

* SHMUH GEH GHEE: a guest at a Passover seder who says he can't stand sweet wine.

78

FORTUNE STRUDEL*

Before you get from the shelf the flour, let us tell you something. Strudel making is not a picnic. So better you should find a nice bakery and buy there your strudel. When you get home from the bakery, you'll take some little pieces paper and write on them fortunes.* You can lie a little, nobody will check up. When all the fortunes are written, you'll put each one on a plate and on the top you'll put a piece strudel. Let a little piece paper stick out from underneath so they'll see it and not eat it together with the strudel. This you'll find nice to serve to the girls for Mah-Jong.

* If you should maybe not have too much imagination . . . here are some ideas for fortunes you can borrow:

You're going to soon get lots of money. However, don't spend it all till you get it . . . I could maybe be wrong.

In two, maybe three months, you'll be getting a new mink. Wear it in good health!

There's a very long trip in your future (probably to Miami); so better you should start getting your clothes together.

There's a tall, handsome man in your future! If you're already married—watch out! If not, Mazeltuv!

Don't be surprised if you get a gift soon. If you don't like it, you can always exchange it.

It's a possibility you might get something exciting in the mail. If it's too exciting, you should maybe report it to the postmaster.

One of the girls at this party doesn't like you. Call me tomorrow and I'll tell you who!

Lil bought the same blouse you're wearing and she paid $5 less for it! But don't say I told you!

Your son Stanley, the plastic surgeon, will be coming home from school soon. Would he like to meet my daughter, Janice?

You're getting a little heavy, dear, in the hips; so maybe you shouldn't take already anymore strudel.

(You can see this dish offers endless possibilities!)

YOU'RE WANTING MAYBE
THE REAL THING?

All of the recipes found in this book have been fixed up so you should be able to buy the ingredients. But maybe you want to be difficult; maybe you want the real thing. Well, if that's the case, then here's a list of some of the substitutes in these recipes and the Chinese things they were substituted for:

Celery	Celery Cabbage (Bok Choy)
Cucumber	Bitter Melon (Fooh Quar Ngow)
Lettuce	Celery Cabbage (Bok Choy)
Mushrooms	Chinese Mushrooms (Dung Goo)
Ginger Powder	Ginger Root (Sang Gueng)
Anise Seed	Star Anise (Bok Gok)

All of the other Chinese things like:

canned bean sprouts	soy sauce
canned water chestnuts	duck sauce
canned bamboo shoots	hot dry mustard

you can get in most supermarkets. However, if you find it's not so easy to get these things in your neighborhood stores, then you should try already the places mentioned below; they'll have them for sure. You can order also from these stores through the mail.

CALIFORNIA
Chong Kee Jan
957 Grant Avenue
San Francisco, California

Shew Hing Lung Co.
832 Grant Avenue
San Francisco, California

Yee Sing Cheng Co.
960 N. Hill Street
Los Angeles, California

ILLINOIS
Sun Wah Hing Trading Co.
2246 S. Wentworth Avenue
Chicago, Illinois

Mee Jun Mercantile Co.
2223 S. Wentworth Avenue
Chicago, Illinois

MASSACHUSETTS
Tai Kwong Co.
60 Beach Street
Boston, Mass.

MICHIGAN
Lun Yick.Co.
1339 Third Avenue
Detroit, Michigan

MISSOURI
Lun Sing Co.
10 South 8th Street
St. Louis, Missouri

NEW YORK
China Food Center
20 East Broadway
N.Y.C.

Wing Fat Co.
35 Mott Street
N.Y.C.

Wo Fat Co.
16 Bowery
N.Y.C.

PENNSYLVANIA
Wing On Co.
1005 Race Street
Philadelphia, Penna.

TEXAS
Chung Mee Co.
712 Franklin Street
Houston, Texas

WASHINGTON, D.C.
Mee Wah Lung Co.
608 "H" Street
Washington, D.C.

INDEX

82

THE ITALIAN-KOSHER COOKBOOK

THE ITALIAN-KOSHER COOKBOOK

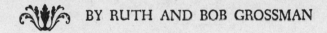 BY RUTH AND BOB GROSSMAN

To the ladies of Hadassah,
God bless them, every one!

Thou shalt not eat any abominable thing . . .

And every beast that parteth the hoof, and cleaveth the cleft into two claws, and chewest the cud among beasts, that ye shall eat . . .

These ye shall eat of all that are in the waters: all that have fins and scales shall ye eat . . .

Of all clean birds ye shall eat . . .

But these are they of which ye shall not eat: the eagle, the ossifrage and the osprey . . . and the glede, and the kite, and the vulture after his kind,

And every raven after his kind . .

And every creeping thing that flieth is unclean unto you: they shall not be eaten . . .

But of all clean fowls ye may eat . . .

Ye shall not eat of any thing that dieth of itself . . . thou shalt not seethe a kid in his mother's milk . . .

DEUTERONOMY XIV

PREFACE

It wasn't too many years ago that Grandma Slipakoff stunned the whole family with her tradition breaking Kosher Chinese recipes . . . . not only the family—the neighbors, and even friends thought this "Chinese kick" would pass. Grandma knew her traditional Kosher dishes were no longer interesting enough to lure "the kids" back home every Friday night.

But Grandma started going overboard. How much Kosher Chinese food can a person eat? EGG ROLL HAH DAH SAH or CHICKEN GOY YIM WITH VEGETABLES are really great, now and then. Even FAH SHTUNK KEN NAH FISH ROLL is a real treat, occasionally. And how often can you eat FAR BLUN JED EGG DROP SOUP?

Then Grandma noticed we started drifting away again. When she'd call us, it was usually, "Noo? So what's the matter? Mine Chinese Kosher cooking's not good enough? You were wanting maybe SHLUMAZOL STUFFED ARTICHOKE?"

This could mean only one thing! Grandma was now involved in

another major campaign . . . this time collecting *Italian* recipes and making them Kosher, so she could present to the family a whole new menu of gourmet delights from which to choose. So, we pulled out the note paper and thought—here we go again! These recipes, just as the Chinese Kosher ones, must be preserved for posterity . . . we have to write another cookbook!

Grandma now actually makes her own spaghetti, except on Shabbos, of course, when she can't cook and we all sit around eating AH BISSEL BORSHT MILANESE.

It's pretty hard these days to hide a smile when she pulls out her own special *espresso* coffee maker . . . . and she's quite proud of her new culinary achievements. We're back in the fold again; and Grandma, happy in her new role of Creator of Kosher Foods of all Nations, is now trying to get Manischewitz to put out "a nice Chianti, it should be dry."

Ruth & Bob Grossman

Brooklyn Heights, N. Y.

viii

TABLE OF ❧ CONTENTS

THE ITALIAN-KOSHER COOKBOOK

SO YOU THINK IT'S ALL SPAGHETTI!

If you ask most people, they'll say that Italian food is pasta, tomato sauce, oregano and garlic. They're right . . . but, there's more to it than that. There are nice veal dishes, chicken fixed all kinds ways, polenta (this is a cornmeal mush they like in Northern Italy), lots of good, healthy vegetables, fish, and even rice sometimes instead of spaghetti. But since most Italian restaurants are run by immigrants from Sicily and Southern Italy, the Italian foods most Americans know are heavy with tomato and meat sauces, Parmesan cheese on almost everything, and all kinds pizza pies and plenty olive oil.

The food in Northern Italy is not so heavy as in Southern Italy. But everywhere they have their favorite pastas, olive oil and such spices! In the North, they're mostly using butter, instead of olive oil—with meat yet! So we're using *parve* oleomargerine where they're using butter. . . .

Some people think Italian food is loaded with garlic. Look, Italians are like everybody else . . . they have things "that just don't agree with me," too. Some like lots of garlic, and some don't. It's better to have not enough than too much anyway. If you're serving garlic to company, just be sure everyone eats it. That way, nobody is offended . . . nobody is offensive.

In Italy they're using wine, but it's not exactly Kosher. In these recipes, you'll find sometimes red, sometimes white wine . . . but always the wines were Kosher, and put out by nice people who really know the Kosher wine business. If you ever go through one of their wineries, it'll take you maybe a few days to sober up . . . but, believe me, when it's all over you'll be a *mayvin* of Kosher wines! *Better you should remember some of these cooking hints:*

In New York there is a manufacturer who makes strictly Kosher Ricotta and Mozzarella cheeses. However, if you can't get these Kosher cheeses in your city, cottage cheese is just like Ricotta, and Muenster cheese melts just like Mozzarella.

If you're using canned tomatoes, you'll put them in a blender and

1

give a few quick blends . . . otherwise, break up with the fork to take out from them the lumps. If you're using fresh tomatoes, put them in boiling water for about 30 seconds. Then peel them and dice them. Use very red, ripe tomatoes. It'll give the sauce such a nice rich color.

When you use capers in your cooking, and if you buy the kind that comes packed in vinegar, you'll be sure to rinse off the capers to remove the extra vinegar. If the capers are for salad or antipasto, why rinse?

Veal cutlets, buy sliced very thin. If the butcher's a nice *haymisha* man, he'll pound them for you, or you can pound yourself with a mallet or even the bottom of a heavy pot.

When you're cooking spaghetti or other pasta, add a tiny splash oil to the cooking water. This way it doesn't all stick together and make such a mess! And you don't have to rinse off with cold water, which —what else?—makes cold the spaghetti.

Don't ever break the spaghetti when you're boiling it, or the lasagne or any long pasta. If your pot seems too small, put part of the pasta in the water, and little by little you'll push with a spoon the rest of it. As it softens, it bends . . . like magic. You shouldn't be embarrassed to twirl long spaghetti on your fork. Just look around and you'll find everyone else is doing it, too. The secret is, you shouldn't start with too much spaghetti. Just don't slurp (not too loud anyway). At least spaghetti is a lot easier than fighting chopsticks!

When cooking sauces, it's better to have a nice heavy bottomed pot. This way the heat is even and there's not so much chance your sauce will stick to your bottom. But now and then you should stir. Stirring is very good for people who don't smoke anymore . . . . and need to do something with their hands. All this and the sauce doesn't stick either!

Italians drink wine the way we drink seltzer . . . . and a meal's not a meal unless you have a nice dry wine. You don't have to get *shicker* at every meal; just have enough in a wine glass to put that nice little touch.

And, finally, there's something about candlelight that makes a delicious Italian meal even better yet. That, plus a glass wine, and maybe a little soft music on the hi-fi, and oy, vay! don't ask!

2

ANTIPASTO

ANTIPASTO*

Every Italian restaurant has antipasto on the menu. This can be everything from lettuce, pimiento, sardines & different kinds sausages and cheese (such a combination you shouldn't know from it!) to stuffed mushrooms, stuffed eggplants, some kind of *hahzarei* they call clams, and lots other stuff. Every restaurant has its own special antipasto . . . some good; some not so good. And over the whole thing you usually pour oil and vinegar. On the next page are suggestions for an antipasto to serve whether you're having *fleischig* or *milchig*. You can use your imagination to add all sorts of other interesting specialties you may have:

4

ANTIPASTO FLEISCHIG

In the list you see here, some things you can get out of a can or at the nearest delicatessen. The ones with asterisks you'll find recipes for on the next few pages.

Cocktail frankfurters
Corned beef slices
Pastrami slices
**Eggs Diablo Alla Tuhmel
Olives (black & green)
Pimiento
Kosher Pickle
Eggplant (comes in jars with vinegar)

**Pickled Mushrooms Facrimta Puhnum
Very thinly sliced corned beef around a wedge of honeydew melon
Parsley sprigs
Chick Peas

ANTIPASTO MILCHIG

You used to call it "tonight we're having dairy." But when you're using this book, it becomes Antipasto Milchig. For this we suggest:

Cheese slices (many varieties)
Soft cheeses
Various smoked fish
Sardines
Anchovies
Olives (black & green)

Pimiento
Eggs stuffed with tuna fish
Celery
Cherry tomatoes
Scallions

* *ANTIPASTO*: what the Italians serve in place of chopped liver.

5

EGGS DIABLO ALLA TUHMEL*

6 hard-boiled eggs
2 teaspoons wine vinegar
1½ tablespoons olive oil

2 small cloves garlic, mashed
1 teaspoon salt
Dash pepper

Cut each egg in half and take out from the whites the yolks, and mash them together with everything else. Now put back into the whites, the yolks . . . but be careful you don't tear the whites . . . an artist you should be in the kitchen.

* *TUHMEL*: the family reaction when Steve announced he was getting his own apartment.

PICKLED MUSHROOMS
FACRIMTA PUHNUM*

1 lb. button mushrooms
1½ cups wine vinegar
½ cup water
1 teaspoon celery seed
A few cloves garlic

1 teaspoon mustard seed
1 teaspoon peppercorns
A few pinches salt
¼ cup olive oil

In a saucepan, you should simmer nice everything but the mushrooms. After 5 minutes of simmering, throw in the mushrooms and for another 5 minutes you'll simmer. Then you can pack good the mushrooms into a sterilized jar and pour in the liquid. If you don't have enough liquid left, it's alright to add a little bit water. Cover the jar tight and put it in a cool place for at least 2 days before you'll serve. This is not only good to use in an antipasto, but it's also good to put in a tossed salad for a little extra *tamm*.

* *FACRIMTA PUHNUM:* Mom's description of the girl who jilted her son, Herbie.

CAPONATA MESHUGENUH PAPPARAZZI*

2 medium eggplants
1½ cups olive oil
2 nice size onions, sliced
1¼ cups canned tomatoes, drained

2 ounces capers, drained
2 tablespoons sugar
¼ cup wine vinegar
A few pinches salt & pepper

First wash nice the eggplants and cut up into small cubes. Then you can fry in the oil until they are soft and a little brown. When they are done, take them out from the pan and drain. Then you can fry nice the onions until they are soft and golden. Put the eggplants and onions in a bowl and throw in the tomatoes and capers. Chop this up a little so there are no big chunks left. Now this whole mess you'll put already into a saucepan, mix together the vinegar and sugar and pour this also in. Add the salt and pepper and let it simmer on the fire for about 20 minutes. Every once in a while make sure to give a stir. Now let it get good and cold. This is a wonderful shmear for crackers at a party, and it's also good when it's part of an antipasto. What you don't use up right away, you'll put in the refrigerator. It keeps for days. Serve this in large amounts, because with this people make from themselves real pigs (you should pardon the expression!)

* *MESHUGENUH PAPPARAZZI*: those crazy Italian photographers who are busy chasing after Italian actresses when they could be photographing some nice Jewish girls.

8

ARTICHOKES JUDAEA
COHN MITZVAH*

As many artichokes as you
need to make 1 per person
A little lemon juice

A pot hot oil
A little salt & pepper

Tell your vegetable man to pick out small and tender artichokes. When you get home, cut off from them the first half inch of the tips and peel nice the stems. Also, you can take off all the tough outside leaves. Now pour a little lemon juice into some water and wash the artichokes in this. After you wash, you'll turn upside down so they'll drain good. (It's a good idea to do this a few hours before you fry. If there's any water left on the artichokes, when you fry, the pot will boil over and make from your kitchen a mess!)

Now make the oil good and hot and fry a few artichokes at a time until they're a nice golden brown. Let them drain and sprinkle with a little salt and pepper. If you like potato chips, you'll like this. This dish is very popular with the Jews in Rome and it's about time everybody knew about it. This everyone will love . . . . . but serve as soon as they're cooked, and don't forget to eat the heart.

* *MITZVAH:* when Sam Cohn donated his Christmas bonus to the *shul.*

SHLUMAZEL STUFFED ARTICHOKE*

This recipe is just for 1 artichoke, but who ever heard of cooking just one? So what you'll do is multiply each amount of the ingredients by the number of artichokes you want to fix. All you'll need is 1 artichoke for each person.

¼ cup bread crumbs
¼ cup grated Parmesan cheese
1 small clove garlic, minced
1 tablespoon fine chopped onions
1 tablespoon chopped parsley

1 teaspoon olive oil
3 tablespoons vegetable broth
A few pinches salt and pepper
A nice dash paprika
1 artichoke

First you should mix together the bread crumbs, cheese, garlic, onions, parsley, olive oil, broth, salt and pepper and paprika. Put this aside and start fixing up the artichokes. Cut off from the tip the first half inch, then cut off the stem, peel off the tough outside leaves, and cut out the choke from the inside. (That's the hairy part.) Now push down the artichoke on the table top so the leaves will spread out a little. The stuffing you should put in the center of the artichoke, although some folks stuff it in between the leaves. You do the way you like best. Now you'll put the artichoke into a saucepan and put in about an inch of water and a pinch salt. Put on tight the cover and let it steam for a half hour or so. It's ready when you can pull out from it easy, a leaf. You can serve artichokes hot or cold, they're so good. When you eat this, be sure to serve knives and don't forget to eat the heart . . . . it's the best part! You'll need extra napkins with this.

* SHLUMAZEL: describes the fellow who when told, "Sorry, next elevator!" answers, "That's the story of my life."

10

PRESSED TUNA ALLA GANTZE MISHPOKHE*

1-7 oz. can salmon
3-7 oz. cans tuna
¼ lb. butter, melted
3 nice fresh beaten eggs

A few good pinches pepper
2 tablespoon chopped parsley
¼ cup drained capers
¼ cup shelled pistachio nuts

Remove first the skins and bones from the can salmon. Now mix it together with the tuna and chop it up, it should be fine. Next you'll mix in the butter, eggs, pepper, parsley and capers. With an electric mixer you should mix for a few minutes so everything is together nice. Then you can throw in the pistachio nuts and mix a little more. Grease good the top part of a double boiler and make in it a lining from wax paper. In this the tuna mish-mash should go. Cook for an hour, and let it cool. While it's cooling you should lay on the top of the tuna a small plate and on this put something heavy, so that the mixture will get pressed good. Put the double boiler top (be sure it's cooled enough) with the weights in the refrigerator to chill. When you're ready to serve, take off from the top the plate and the weights and put the double boiler top in hot water for a few minutes. Now you can take it out. On a plate you'll turn it upside down, and let the pressed tuna fall out. One thing you shouldn't forget, peel off the wax paper before you serve. And maybe you can give a little squeeze of lemon juice on top. This makes more than enough to serve for Mah Jong or Bocci or whatever the girls play.

* GANTZE MISHPOKHE: the family Board of Directors who tell you what you want to be when you grow up, and with whom!

STUFFED EGGPLANT
INDIGESTIONE*

1 small eggplant
1 small onion, chopped
1 clove garlic, minced
1 teaspoon oregano
2 tablespoons olive oil
A few pinches salt

½ cup bread crumbs
1 beaten egg
A little chopped parsley
A little grated Parmesan
cheese

Bake first the eggplant in a medium oven for 30 minutes or until it looks like somebody let the air out from it. Then you can cut it into 4 wedges and scoop out from it, the insides. Don't forget to save the skins. Now you can sauté the onion, garlic and oregano in 1 tablespoon of the oil until they get soft. Mix this together with the eggplant insides (make sure there are no lumps), the salt and the bread crumbs. Then you can add the beaten egg and the other tablespoon oil. Mix together nice and stuff into the eggplant skins. On top you can sprinkle a little of the chopped parsley and Parmesan cheese. Put them under the broiler for 10 or 15 minutes and they're done. Makes enough for 3 or 4 people, they should have hearty appetites!

* *INDIGESTIONE:* the Italian answer to Jewish heartburn.

12

STUFFED MUSHROOMS
ALLA MOHEL*

1 tablespoon anise seed	½ cup melted oleo
½ cup water	A little splash hot sauce
1 tight packed cup spinach	A nice pinch salt
¼ cup also tight parsley	3 anchovies, mashed
1 medium onion	½ cup bread crumbs

About 2 dozen nice mushroom caps

Simmer first the anise seed in the water for 10 minutes, then throw away the seeds and keep the water. In a blender add the anise seed water, the spinach, parsley, onion and melted oleo. Blend it all together so it should be smooth. Now mix in the hot sauce, salt, and smashed anchovies. Put this in a little saucepan and simmer for 10 or 12 minutes. Afterwards, you'll throw in the bread crumbs. When it's mixed nice together, heap up good in each mushroom cap some of the stuffing and put them under the broiler for 10 to 15 minutes. Serve it hot to your guests and, believe me, they'll lick their fingers. (Better that, than wipe them on your tablecloth.)

* *MOHEL:* a surgeon who performs only at parties.

KOKKAPITZZI PIZZA
WITH LOX*

YOU NEED A NICE DOUGH:

1 package yeast   2 tablespoons oil
⅞ cup water, warmed   2⅔ cups flour, sifted

A pinch salt

First you'll add the yeast to the warm water and let it soften. Then add the salt, oil and flour. Knead for 5 minutes until it gets smooth and a little rubbery, and you get a little tired. Brush it with a little oil and put it in a bowl. Cover the bowl with a cloth and let it stand in a warm place, like maybe by the radiator, for about 2 hours until the dough gets twice as big.

MEANWHILE, YOU'LL MAKE THE SAUCE:

2 tablespoons oil   1 cup water
2 medium onions, chopped   Salt and pepper, enough to
fine   taste
1-6 oz. can tomato paste

Sauté good the onions for about 5 minutes. Then you'll add the tomato paste and the water. Also the salt and pepper. Let this simmer uncovered 15 minutes, while you sit and have a sip of coffee.

14

NOW FOR THE OTHER STUFF:

1 tablespoon olive oil	½ cup lox in shreds
1 cup Mozzarella cheese, sliced thin	A little oregano

When the dough has grown to double its size, you can knead it again on a floury board and spread it out into a large 14 inch circle. Now take a 14 or 15 inch flat pan and smear on it a little olive oil. Spread out the dough in the pan and put plenty of the sauce on it, you should cover all over. Now put on the tablespoon olive oil and sprinkle on the Mozzarella. Put on the pieces lox (you can also use mushrooms and/or anchovies) and sprinkle on the oregano. Now you can put the whole thing into a 500° oven and let it bake for 15 or 20 minutes until the edges turn a little brown and the cheese is bubbling. Slice it up in wedges and serve. If you want that real pizzeria atmosphere, the only way to do it is buy a jukebox and invite lots of teen-agers; but, believe me, pizza with lox they won't find at the neighborhood Pizza Palace!

* KOKKAPITZZI: a Southern Yiddish word meaning everything but the kitchen stove, which is optional.

LEONARDO DA VINCI
GARLIC BREAD*

1 long loaf Italian bread	Salt & pepper, 'til it tastes
2 cloves garlic, minced	like something
½ cup olive oil	Maybe a sprinkle paprika
	for color

In a saucepan, warm up the olive oil and the garlic and salt and pepper. Now you'll cut the bread like you're going to slice it, only don't cut all the way. (Later you'll see how easy it'll be to tear off each slice.) Now shmear the heated mixture in each slit, sprinkle on the paprika, and wrap the whole loaf in foil and put it in the oven. If you're cooking other things in the oven and it's very hot, the bread should be done in no time at all. Just keep an eye on it. But if you check it, use a thick potholder so you don't get burned from the heat. Otherwise, cook at 375° about 15 minutes. Tonight you'll be generous with the garlic ... tomorrow, the mouthwash!

* *LEONARDO DA VINCI:* "my son the painter, the mathematician, the mechanic, the inventor, the anatomist, the sculptor, the scientist, the architect, the engineer. . . . . . ."

SOUPS

MINESTRONE DELLA CONTESSA GOLDFARB*

2 tablespoons olive oil
2 nice onions, chopped
2 quarts meat stock
1 cup cut up string beans
2 tablespoons tomato paste
1 nice handful spinach, torn up
1 tablespoon parsley, chopped
2 chopped up carrots
1 can kidney beans

2 small zucchini, sliced
2 medium potatoes, diced
¼ small cabbage, shredded
Enough salt & pepper so it will have a taste
1 tablespoon MSG
1 cup Tubettini (Macaroni #42)
A little extra stock to pour in, if you need

Put in a nice big pot the oil and sauté the onions until they get soft. Then the meat stock you can throw in (if you made flanken more often, then maybe you'd have meat stock) and then the rest of the ingredients, but not the Tubettini. Cover the pot and let it cook for ½ hour. Now you can throw in the Tubettini and a little more stock if the soup is too thick. Let it cook for another 20 minutes and it's ready to serve to an army. But don't worry, it keeps nice in the refrigerator. Serves 1 Army.

* *LA CONTESSA GOLDFARB*: the Italian Jennie Grossinger.

AH BISSEL BORSHT MILANESE*

10 medium sized beets	½ teaspoon pepper
10 cups vegetable bouillon	1 tablespoon sugar
4 ripe tomatoes, peeled & diced	1 cup cream
	¼ cup flour
1 tablespoon lemon juice	2 eggs
1 tablespoon salt	

Wash, peel and slice nice the beets. Put the bouillon and beets in a large pot, cover and bring to a boil. Make low the heat, and simmer until the beets are nice and tender and everything good has been cooked out of them. Meantime, you'll put the tomatoes in a blender with lemon juice, salt, pepper, sugar, the sour cream and flour. When it's all blended nice so there are no lumps in the mish-mash, pour it slowly into the soup, stirring constantly. Now you'll cool it. Some people like it hot; but to most people, there's no borsht like cold borsht. When the soup is cooled, you should blend in slowly the eggs. This will be the most unusual borsht you ever had . . . who ever heard of borsht with tomatoes in it? But listen, who ever heard of an Italian-Kosher Cookbook? This makes a pot that'll serve the family for days. With all the beets that are left over, you can serve them as a vegetable with a little margerine or you can marinate them, in vinegar and pickling spices.

* AH BISSEL BORSHT: what Mrs. Michelangelo put in her son's thermos everyday when he was working at the Sistine Chapel.

MAMA LEVY'S VENDETTA LENTIL SOUP*

3 quarts water
1 lb. lentils
3 tablespoons olive oil
1 clove garlic, minced
1 onion, chopped
1 stalk celery, diced

1 cup canned tomatoes
A few pinches salt & pepper,
   to taste
A few sprinkles Parmesan
   cheese

Cook the lentils in 3 quarts boiling water for about 1 hour and 15 minutes. While this is cooking, you'll brown lightly in olive oil the garlic, onion and celery. When the lentils are through cooking, strain them through a sieve with the tomatoes. Add now a cup of water or enough to make the soup as thick or as thin as you like it and the salt and pepper. Then put in the garlic, onion and celery and simmer for 10 minutes. When you serve the soup, you can sprinkle a little cheese on top (depending what the rest of the meal is). This makes enough for 6 people, with some left over for a nice nosh for tomorrow.

* MAMA LEVY'S VENDETTA: wait 'til your father comes home —then you'll get it!

20

ZUPPA DI ESCAROLE
GOYISHA KUPP*

6 cups nice chicken soup	1 chopped onion
2 tablespoons tomato paste	1 chopped carrot
2 teaspoons salt	1 cup diced celery
A little bit pepper	2 cups pasta shells

4 cups shredded escarole

Mix everything together in a nice soup pot, except the pasta shells and the escarole, and simmer for about a half hour. Now bring to a boil and add the shells and escarole and continue cooking until the shells are done. Take one of the shells and give a little chew to see if it's tender . . . it takes about 15 minutes. And, believe it or not, that's all there is to it. You'll have to decide for yourself how many it serves, because everybody's soup bowls are different.

* *GOYISHA KUPP:* he thinks a "shofar" is someone who drives a Rolls Royce.

SALADS & DRESSINGS

SHNORRA STRING BEAN SALAD*

6 tablespoons olive oil
3 tablespoons wine vinegar
A few pinches salt & pepper
1 chopped onion

1 lb. string beans, cooked &
drained
4 hard-boiled eggs, chopped
3 tablespoons mayonnaise

1 teaspoon prepared mustard

Anyone can make easily this dish. It's mostly just mixing different things together. You mix the olive oil, wine vinegar, salt and pepper, and onion. Then add all this to the drained string beans and chill awhile. When you take it out from the refrigerator, you'll mix (again with the mixing!) the chopped eggs with mayonnaise and mustard. A drop of vinegar in this adds a nice *tamm*. Cover this egg mixture and chill it. When it's ready to serve, you'll spoon the string bean mixture on plates covered with lettuce, and on top of this you'll put the egg mixture. If company's coming over, this can be finished even before they ring the doorbell. It's enough for 4 salads. If you're having more, you'll fix more.

* *SHNORRA*: sees his dentist twice a year to read all the magazines he "can't afford."

23

EXCITING DRESSINGS SO YOU SHOULDN'T SERVE NEBISH SALADS*

ANCHOVY DRESSING

4 anchovies
½ cup olive oil

3 tablespoons wine vinegar
A little pepper

Mash the anchovies to a paste . . . don't cheat . . . . . be sure it's very mashed. Then you'll add the rest of the ingredients and mix everything all up.

ITALIAN CHEESE DRESSING

¼ cup olive oil
3 tablespoons wine vinegar

A few pinches salt & pepper
¼ cup grated cheese

You'll mix nice all the ingredients and blend it very good. Better you should put a sticker on it saying "Cheese" or you might make a very embarrassing mistake.

24

OIL AND VINEGAR DRESSING

⅓ cup wine vinegar
1 clove garlic, mashed
6 tablespoons olive oil

A little salt & pepper
A couple pinches oregano

Put this all in a jar or bottle and give a few healthy shakes. Let it stand overnight in the refrigerator, then the next day you've got some tasty dressing!

GORGONZOLA DRESSING

1 nice minced piece garlic
½ teaspoon dry mustard
A little pinch salt

¼ cup olive oil
½ cup wine vinegar
3 oz. Gorgonzola cheese

If you've got a blender, throw in everything and blend. If you don't have one (what's the matter, you can't save stamps?), mash everything together with a fork. This dressing you can also make with Roquefort cheese, but Gorgonzola is much cheaper and just as good. This is a good dressing to serve on cold string beans, cannelloni, chick peas or even lettuce.

* NEBISH: on his trip to Italy, he tried to get hotel reservations in Pompeii.

JULIUS CAESAR SALAD
ALLA GAHTKUS*

1 clove garlic, minced
2 strips anchovy, mashed
A pinch pepper & salt
2 tablespoons salad oil
2½ tablespoons vinegar
4 tablespoons mayonnaise (or yoghurt, if you're zoftik)

1 teaspoon Parmesan cheese
A sprig or so of parsley
1 raw egg (when you mix it up, nobody can tell)
Romaine
Croutons (before serving)

There are 2 ways you can make this salad. One is to make the salad dressing by mixing good together everything but the croutons and romaine. Some folks feel funny about serving a raw egg and cook it just a few seconds. But, believe me, that's just extra work and extra dishes to wash. Like when you put a raw egg in a malt, who can tell? When you're ready to serve the salad, you'll pour the dressing over the torn romaine leaves and throw in some croutons to help soak up that delicious dressing.

26

But if you want to be fancy, you can rub a nice size salad bowl with the minced garlic (a wooden bowl is better for this), then mash very nice with a fork the anchovies. Now you'll sprinkle the salt and pepper. Mix it all up and pour on the salad oil, vinegar and mayonnaise (or yoghurt). With a fork you'll give everything a nice few healthy stirs. Now put in the cheese, parsley and that egg. You'll give one more nice mix to everything and for an extra treat, lick the fork before you put it in the sink. Cover the salad bowl and put it in the refrigerator. Later, when you're ready to serve the salad, put the romaine in the bowl with the dressing, throw on the croutons and toss.

You'd better have extra copies of this recipe, because whenever anyone serves this salad, everybody always says, "For this I want the recipe before I leave." The egg you can tell them about at the door when you're saying goodbye.

* *GAHTKUS*: what Julius Caesar's mother made him wear under his toga on cold days.

ARTICHOKE SALAD CON OLIVIA OLIO*

1 package frozen artichoke hearts
A pinch salt
A pinch pepper
2 tablespoons wine vinegar

6 tablespoons olive oil
A little clove garlic, crushed
A pinch sugar
Some romaine

Boil nice the frozen artichoke hearts and put them in the refrigerator, they should get cold. Meantime, you'll mix together all the other things (except the romaine). Now you can take out from the refrigerator the artichokes and put them on a few pieces nice romaine. If there's room in your refrigerator, you'll have the salad on the plates all ready to serve. Pour on the sauce just before you put the salads on the table. This should be enough for about 4 people, who, you'll be sure, like artichoke hearts.

* OLIVIA OLIO: Italian chicken *shmaltz*.

28

EGG & MATZOH DISHES

EGGS DON GIOVANNI
IZZAH GOY*

1 cup tomato sauce
1 tablespoon chopped parsley
A nice pinch garlic powder
A pinch salt & pepper
½ teaspoon oregano

8 slices white bread
A little olive oil
8 slices Mozzarella cheese
4 nice eggs

Mix nice together in a saucepan the tomato sauce, parsley, garlic powder, salt, pepper and oregano. Now let this simmer for 10 minutes and then put it aside. Take out your baking pan and lay in it 4 slices of the bread. Brush on a little olive oil, put on each piece 2 slices of cheese and spread on the tomato sauce mixture. The other 4 slices bread you'll press out from the center a hole using a water tumbler. Put these on top of the other slices to make sandwiches and also brush with a little oil. Now you can bake in the oven at 325° until the cheese melts. Meanwhile, poach in a little salted water the eggs and when the "sandwiches" are done, put the poached eggs in the little pressed out hole. Serve this to 4 people, nice and hot. But if you're very hungry, you should fix 2 sandwiches per person; and if you're still hungry, maybe you should have eaten out tonight.

* *DON GIOVANNI:* the only one on Grandma's block with a Christmas tree.

OMELET ALLA GRAND
CONCOURSE*

2 tablespoons olive oil
3 medium onions, chopped
1 clove garlic, chopped
1 cup canned drained tomatoes
¾ cup chopped mushrooms

A few pinches salt
A little pinch pepper
1 tablespoon chopped parsley
1 teaspoon oregano
6 nice fresh eggs

In a little saucepan you'll put the onions and garlic and sauté until they get soft. Then you'll put in the tomatoes, mushrooms, salt, pepper, parsley and oregano. Let this simmer for 20 minutes. While you're simmering, you can beat up nice the eggs with a little salt and pepper. When the filling is almost ready you'll put a little oil into a nice large frying pan and make a big omelet. Now put the omelet on a platter and pour on one side the filling. The egg now, you should fold over the filling and cut it up into portions so you can serve. This makes a nice Sunday breakfast for 4 people, especially if you've got company. Serve with or without toasted bagels, depending on what time you're serving lunch.

* GRAND CONCOURSE: The Jewish Appian Way.

UM GEPAHTCH KID MATZOH BREI PARMIGIANA*

6 matzohs
1 chopped onion
1 clove garlic, chopped
1 tablespoon olive oil
2 cups tomato sauce
1 tablespoon parsley,
  chopped

A couple pinches salt
A little pepper
5 nice fresh eggs
½ cup diced Mozzarella
  cheese

Soak first the matzohs in water so they'll be soft. While you're soaking, you can sauté the onion and garlic in the olive oil until they brown a little. Then put them into a saucepan and add the tomato sauce, parsley, salt and pepper. Let this simmer good for 20 minutes. Now you can drain the matzohs by squeezing out from them the water. Mix them together with the eggs, salt and pepper and put half of this mess into an oiled casserole. Sprinkle over this, half the cheese and then the rest of the matzoh mixture. Sprinkle on the rest of the cheese and pour on the top the tomato sauce. Now you'll put the casserole uncovered into a 325° oven and let it cook for 25 minutes. This will be almost as fluffy as a soufflé and will surprise 5-6 people.

* *UM GEPAHTCH KID*: those snazzy new cars from Detroit with everything from gold plated hub caps to "his" and "her" safety belts.

PASTA & OTHER STARCHES

MANICOTTI CON RICOTTA DI MIA BUBBA*

FIRST, THE SAUCE:

4 tablespoons olive oil
2 cloves garlic, minced
1 medium onion, chopped fine
2 tablespoons chopped parsley

2-1 lb. cans tomatoes
1-8 oz. can tomato sauce
Salt & pepper, you should taste
1 teaspoon sugar
½ teaspoon basil

Sauté in olive oil the garlic, onion, and parsley until the onion and garlic look golden. Then add the rest of the ingredients and simmer uncovered 'til it's thick . . . about 20 minutes.

Now you'll make ready the Manicotti and the stuffing while the sauce cooks. But keep an eye on it, you should stir now and then. You know what they say: "A watched pot cooks maybe a little faster."

NOW THE MANICOTTI:

Cook the Manicotti (which looks like very healthy spaghetti) in a pot boiling salted water, with 1 tablespoon olive oil, so it shouldn't all stick together . . . *only cook 'til it's half-done,* about 12 minutes. (If you forget to do this, you can forget all about it, and fix tuna fish tonight.) Then you should drain and rinse in cold water. Put the Manicotti aside and you're ready for:

34

FINALLY, THE CHEESE FILLING:

1 lb. Ricotta cheese
¼ lb. Mozzarella cheese, sliced thin
¼ cup grated Parmesan cheese

1½ teaspoons sugar
2 eggs, beaten nice
A few pinches salt & pepper

Mix everything together—it won't hurt you to use your hands, but don't forget to beat first the eggs. Fill up the half-cooked Manicotti (one whole box has 12 pieces) with a teaspoon. Pour a little sauce in the bottom of a baking dish or pan and put the filled Manicotti side by side in one row. Now pour some sauce over the Manicotti and then sprinkle lots of Parmesan cheese on top. If you have to make another layer, be sure to put the sauce on top and then some more Parmesan cheese. Put this in an oven heated already to 350° and cook maybe 30 minutes. (The *goyem* make this with a meat filling, too. For that we wouldn't think of even telling you the recipe. You'll have to look someplace else—like maybe the library where the neighbors won't see.)

* *RICOTTA DI MIA BUBBA:* Grandma's cottage cheese she brings to eat when she visits her *goyisha* friends.

RAVIOLI GALITZIANA*

YOU'LL MAKE FIRST THE DOUGH:

1½ cups flour	A little pinch salt
1 nice fresh egg	1 tablespoon water

First you'll pour on a bread board the flour in a little pile. Now with your finger, make a little hole. Beat up nice the egg and drop it in the hole with the salt and the water. Next you should work it with your fingers and maybe a fork until it gets stiff. Then knead it with your hands a little bit. When it's smooth, cover it up and let it stand for 10 minutes. While you're waiting, it's a good idea to look for your rolling pin. It's probably not where you thought it was. Now, after the 10 minutes are up and you've found the rolling pin, you can cut the dough in half and roll each piece so it gets nice and thin.

NOW FOR THE FILLING:

1 cup ground cooked meat or chicken	½ clove chopped garlic
1 fresh egg, beaten up	2 tablespoons bread crumbs
A few pinches salt	1 tablespoon parve margerine
A few pinches chopped parsley	

36

Mix nice together all these things and put a teaspoonful of it on 1 piece of the dough. Keep putting on teaspoonsful 2 inches apart from each other until all of the filling is used. Then you'll take the other piece dough and cover the whole thing up. With your fingers you can press around each little pile of filling so that the dough sticks together and also makes a little square. Now you can cut the squares apart with a little cookie cutter. Make hot a pot water with a little salt in it and when it's boiling good, put in the ravioli and for 10 minutes you should cook and then drain it. We recommend you pour over it the TO-MATO SAUCE ALLA HEIM SHMEEL (see page 46). Some folks would call this *kreplach* . . . but so you should be modern, you call it ravioli. Serves 5, maybe 6 people.

* *GALITZIANA*: the Jewish equivalent of a Sicilian.

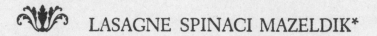 LASAGNE SPINACI MAZELDIK*

1 lb. spinach	1 lb. Ricotta cheese
2 cloves garlic, chopped	2 teaspoons salt
3 tablespoons parsley	A few pinches pepper
1 tablespoon basil	1-10 oz. package Lasagne
1 teaspoon oregano	½ cup grated Parmesan
1 cup bread crumbs	cheese
1-1 lb. can tomatoes	½ lb. Mozzarella cheese
1-6 oz. can tomato paste	1 cup tomato sauce

Rinse good the spinach and put in a pot with a little water. Put on the cover and cook for a few minutes until it's done. Then put the spinach with the garlic, 1 tablespoon parsley, basil and oregano altogether in a blender, or chop it good so it's fine. Now mix in the bread crumbs, tomatoes and the tomato paste. Put this on the side so you'll have room to work on the other stuff. Next you'll take the Ricotta and mix in the salt, pepper, and 2 tablespoons parsley. Put this also on the side; in a minute or two you'll need plenty room. On the package Lasagne you'll see some directions on how you should cook. The only thing we can add is you should cook in a large roasting pan so the noodles can stretch out and not break. Also, add a little spoon oil in the water so the noodles they shouldn't stick together. When it's all done, you'll start to put it together. Grease a little bit the bottom of a baking pan and put in a layer Lasagne noodles, then put in a layer of spinach mixture, then a layer of Ricotta, sprinkle on a little Parmesan cheese and some of the Mozzarella cheese in thin slices. Then you'll put on top another layer noodles and start spreading the other stuff like you just did before. Keep doing this until everything is all used up, but make sure you finish up with a layer of the spinach mixture. On top of this, put a little Mozzarella and a cup tomato sauce. (If you didn't listen and you finished up with noodles, it's *your* teeth that'll break. You'll see how hard those noodles can get!) When everything is all put together the right way, you'll pop into the oven and bake for ½ hour at 375°. This will serve 6 average people or 4 people who, "never eat spicy food, but maybe I'll have just a taste."

* *SPINACI MAZELDIK:* it's lucky we had the spinach to replace the meat in this recipe; otherwise, there'd be no Lasagne!

HUMUTZDIK POLENTA SQUARES*

2 tablespoons olive oil
1 clove garlic, chopped
½ cup celery, diced
1 medium onion, chopped
1 quart water

1 cup cornmeal, yellow
2 teaspoons salt
2 or 3 tablespoons Parmesan
cheese, optional

Enough parve oleo to dot

Sauté in the olive oil until it's nice and brown the garlic, celery and onion. While this is sautéeing, boil good the water and add slow the cornmeal, mixing all the time so you shouldn't get lumpy. When it's all mixed and smooth, into a double boiler you'll put it together with the sautéed vegetables and the salt. Now cover it up and let it double boil for about ½ hour until it gets thick. When it's thick enough, pour it into a greased 10 x 14 inch pan and let it cool. When it's cool, cut it into 1½ inch squares and sprinkle with the Parmesan cheese. Now dot each square with a little oleo and put it into a 400° oven for 20 to 25 minutes to get a little brown. If you're *fleischig* leave out the Parmesan. It'll still be good. This makes enough polenta for 5 to 6 people, and it's a nice change from potatoes or rice.

* *HUMUTZDIK*: pizza at the Passover table.

40

SHMUTZIK RICE WITH CHICKEN LIVERS*

1⅓ cups raw rice
1 cup cooked, diced chicken livers
2 medium onions, chopped
2 nice cloves garlic, chopped
1 diced green pepper

3 tablespoons olive oil
3 chopped up scallions
1 tablespoon parsley flakes
Enough salt & pepper so it should taste like something

Cook the rice nice, it shouldn't stick together, but you'll be sure to turn off the fire a little before it's finished. While this is cooking, sauté the onion, garlic and pepper in olive oil until they're nice and brown. Add this to the almost cooked rice. Now you can also add the diced chicken livers, salt & pepper, the scallions and the parsley. Put a little dot here and there with margerine and cover and cook for 15 minutes in a 350° oven. This makes 5 or 6 portions you won't be ashamed of and it's a sneaky way to make the kids eat liver.

* SHMUTZIK: refers to the "scenic" postcards Dave brought back from Naples.

41

RISOTTO ALLA SHABBOS GOY*

1 tablespoon olive oil
1 large onion, chopped
2 ribs celery, chopped
1 clove garlic, minced
2 cups raw rice

3 cups vegetable or chicken broth
A little salt to taste
A pinch or 2 pepper

Sauté in the oil the onion, celery and garlic until it's a little golden. You'll throw in the rice and make low the fire. Stir this good until the rice turns yellow. Now, you can add the broth, salt and pepper, put on the cover, and cook on a low flame for 30 minutes or until the rice is nice and tender. This will be plenty for 4 to 6 people and it's not as fattening as Potato Kugel.

* SHABBOS GOY: the "Friday nighter lamplighter" who knows more Jewish words than you do.

SAUCES

MEAT SAUCE MONA
LISENBAUM*

2 tablespoons olive oil	A good few pinches salt
2 cloves garlic, chopped	A pinch pepper
1 cup onions, diced	1 teaspoon oregano
1 cup green pepper, diced	2 nice bay leaves
1 cup celery, chopped	1-6 oz. can tomato paste
1 lb. nice ground beef	1-1 lb. can peeled tomatoes

1 cup dry red wine or water (live it up and use wine!)

First you'll brown with the oil the garlic, onions, celery and green pepper. Then throw in the chopped meat and also let it brown. Mix in all the other stuff and let it cook on a nice low fire for an hour. When it's done, serve on top of spaghetti. This is plenty for 4 or 5 people. Serve with this a big green salad and garlic bread and, you'll see, the kids won't be running off all the time to the corner Pizzeria.

* *MONA LISENBAUM:* Mona Lisa's name before the family left Poland.

MARINARA SAUCE
CRISTOFORO COLOMBO*

2 tablespoons olive oil	A little pinch salt
2 nice onions, sliced	A little pinch pepper
2 cloves garlic	A pinch sugar
2-1 lb. cans peeled tomatoes	A little pinch oregano
A few anchovies	2 ozs. Parmesan cheese

Sauté nice the onion and garlic in the olive oil until it's golden. Take out from the pan the garlic and put in next the tomatoes and simmer for an hour. Then put in the anchovies cut in small pieces, the salt, pepper, sugar and oregano. Cook for 10 minutes more and serve over a pound of cooked spaghetti. Don't forget to sprinkle on the cheese. This will be enough for 4 or 5 people if they don't overdo it.

* CRISTOFORO COLOMBO: my son, the discoverer.

TOMATO SAUCE ALLA
HEIM SHMEEL*

2 tablespoons olive oil
3 chopped cloves garlic
3 nice chopped onions
3 tablespoons chopped parsley
2-1 lb. cans tomatoes
1-6 oz. can tomato paste

¼ cup dry red wine
A good few pinches salt to taste
A pinch or 2 ground pepper
1 teaspoon oregano
1 bay leaf

Make hot a saucepan with the oil and cook the garlic and onions until they are soft. Then you'll throw in the rest of the stuff and put the cover on the pot. Now you'll simmer for 2 hours. If the sauce is a little too thin for you, take off from the pot the cover for the last half hour. When it's finished take out the bay leaf and it's ready to serve. It makes about 6 cups and is perfect for *milchidig* spaghetti, all kinds ravioli, or just plain *luckshen*.

* *HEIM SHMEEL*: the Jewish John Doe.

FISH

GEFILLTE FISH FRA DIAVOLO*

8 nice pieces gefillte fish

Is there a *bubba* in the house? Or maybe nearby? If there is, ask her if she would please make the gefillte fish for you. Nobody makes gefillte fish like a *bubba* does. If you're not so lucky, or if *bubba* is in Florida when you decide to make this, you'll find the kind that comes in jars is almost as good, and a lot less trouble. So let's say you already have the fish. Here's what you need to make it FRA DIAVOLO:

2 tablespoons olive oil	2 tablespoons parsley,
3 cloves garlic, chopped	chopped
2 cups canned plum toma-	1 teaspoon oregano
toes	¼ teaspoon crushed red pep-
2 tablespoons vinegar	per seeds
1 teaspoon basil	A little salt

Brown good the garlic in the olive oil in a saucepan. Mash up the tomatoes and put together with the garlic and all the other stuff. Be careful when you put the fish in, they shouldn't break. Now you can let the whole thing simmer for 10 minutes and it's ready to serve. Nobody ever serves gefillte fish as a main dish, so you be different. Spaghetti would be very nice with this to cover with some of that good, hot sauce.

* *GEFILLTE FISH:* in every Jewish home there's a *mezuzah* on the doorpost and this in the refrigerator.

FASHTUNKENA FILET
OF SOLE FIRENZE*

1½ lb. filet of sole	¼ teaspoon pepper
½ cup flour	6 tablespoons butter
1 teaspoon salt	2 cloves garlic, minced

Dust good the fish in the flour mixed together with the salt and pepper. Now you can fry it in the butter until one side is a nice golden brown. Then turn it over and get the other side the same color, they should match. Take out from the pan the fish, and put the pieces in a heated serving dish. Add the garlic to the leftover butter in the pan, sauté it for 2 minutes and pour the whole thing over the fish. Now you'll decorate with some parsley and a few wedges lemon, you should be fancy. Serves 4. This, I'll guarantee you, is an easy dish to make, and such flavor you'll pay plenty for when you eat out!

* *FASHTUNKENA:* Venice at low tide.

QVELLING COD FILETS*

A little butter
1 small onion, sliced like paper
¾ cup dry white wine
2 lbs. cod filets (4 pieces)
A little olive oil for brushing

Some Parmesan cheese for sprinkling
Some bread crumbs, also for sprinkling
A little parsley, chopped
2 teaspoons flour
A pinch salt
½ cup milk

Smear light a baking dish with the butter and the onion slices you'll put in, in one layer. Then you can pour in the wine, (also you can take a little sip yourself; it's good for the appetite). Put in the 4 pieces cod and with a little olive oil you'll brush. Sprinkle on some Parmesan cheese and then some bread crumbs. Now top it off with the chopped parsley and the whole thing you'll bake uncovered in a 350° oven for about 20 minutes, or until it flakes nice. Meanwhile, the flour, salt and milk you'll mix together and heat and stir until it gets thick. When the fish is ready, pour the liquid from the baking dish into the flour-milk mixture and you'll cook until the whole thing thickens a little. Pour it over the fish and serve. This is a good dish to serve to your Catholic friends if they should come to visit on Friday. Serves 4 friends if you also fill them up with a nice vegetable, and maybe a salad with one of those cheese dressings.

* QVELLING: Mom's pride when she finds out her new daughter-in-law is going to keep Kosher.

FRAYLIKHA FISH STEW*

1 lb. cod
1 lb. flounder filets
1 lb. halibut
1 tablespoon olive oil
1 large onion, sliced
2 cloves garlic, chopped
2 ribs celery, diced
1-1 lb. can plum tomatoes
1-8 oz. can tomato sauce
1 tablespoon lemon juice
½ cup mushrooms

1 package frozen zucchini
1 tablespoon parsley, chopped
1 cup water
1 teaspoon basil
1 teaspoon thyme
A good few pinches salt
¼ teaspoon crushed red pepper seeds
1 teaspoon MSG

First you should remove all the skin and bones from the fish; but don't throw them away—in this recipe, there's no waste. Now cut up the pieces fish into little bite sizes. You can sauté until they're soft the onions, garlic and celery. Put these together with the fish into a large nice looking pot. If you listened and still have the skin and bones from the fish, you'll tie them up in a clean piece cloth, and put in the pot. Now all the other stuff you'll put in also and then cover. Simmer for 20 to 25 minutes. When it's all ready, be sure to throw away the cloth. Imagine what the folks at the table would say if you served them fish skin and bones wrapped up in a wet *shmatah*. Now you're ready to serve with mounds of fluffy rice, and this colorful stew will be enough for 7 or 8 people—and maybe some left for tomorrow.

* *FRAYLIKHA*: describes the day Arnie told the folks he was giving up the Peace Corps to become a doctor.

MEATS

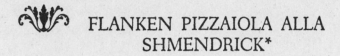

FLANKEN PIZZAIOLA ALLA SHMENDRICK*

FIRST YOU'LL NEED SOME BOILED BEEF:

3 lbs. nice beef to boil
4 quarts water
2 stalks celery
2 nice onions with cloves
   stuck in

A couple sprigs parsley
A little handful salt
A few peppercorns
1 bay leaf
1 tomato

Put everything together in a pot and bring it to a good boil. Then you'll simmer for 3 hours with the cover on. Take out from the pot the beef and cut it in thick slices. The broth you should strain and put away for minestrone or something. The vegetables you'll throw away, such soaked out things you don't need.

NOW FOR THE PIZZAIOLA SAUCE:

2 tablespoons olive oil
2 cloves garlic, sliced
1-1 lb. can tomatoes
1-6 oz. can tomato paste

A pinch or two salt
A good pinch pepper
½ teaspoon oregano
1 tablespoon parsley

Brown first the garlic in the olive oil. Then put in the tomatoes, tomato paste, salt, pepper, oregano, and parsley. Cook on a medium fire for about 15 minutes. If you boiled the beef maybe yesterday and it's cold, you can throw in the pieces in the sauce and let them get hot together. This is a wonderful new way to serve a piece flanken and it's enough for 4 or 5 people . . . it depends on what time they had lunch.

* SHMENDRICK: he invites a date to a formal and takes her there on a subway.

GEHACKTA BEEF DI
MAMA MIA*

1 lb. ground beef	¼ cup olive oil
6 thin strips pimiento	2-8 oz. cans tomato sauce
6 slices salami, shredded	2 tablespoons parsley
1 beaten egg	A few pinches oregano
A few pinches salt	A few pinches garlic
A few pinches pepper	powder
A little flour	1 teaspoon sugar

Spread the beef out on a floury board and pat it out until it's about a half inch thick. Now you'll sprinkle on the strips pimiento, and salami. Pour over this the beaten egg and a little salt and pepper. Now roll it up already like a strudel and dust a little flour on the outside. Put the oil in a good size casserole and brown the meat roll on all sides. Be careful how you're handling; it can fall apart very easy. After you brown, you can next pour on the tomato sauce and throw in the parsley and the rest of the "pinches" and sugar. Let it simmer without a cover for a half hour. If the sauce gets a little too thick for you, it's alright to add a little water or even wine if you like. Skim off the fat. Serves 4 people. (If you don't have 4 people to serve, invite in the kids on the front stoop.)

* *MAMA MIA*: her name is Giacobbi instead of Jacobs; she makes minestrone instead of chicken soup; and she cooks with olive oil instead of shmaltz.

SALTIMBOCCA ALTE KAHKA*

1½ lbs. very thin veal (in 3x4 inch pieces)
¼ cup flour
A few pinches salt
A pinch pepper
¼ cup olive oil

A very thin corned beef slice for each piece veal
2 hard cooked eggs, halved
4 green olives, pitted
½ cup broth
2 tablespoons sherry

Pound first the veal so it should be good and thin. Now mix together the flour, salt and pepper and dredge in this the veal pieces. Now you can brown these in the olive oil. Don't forget to turn them over and brown both sides. When this is finished, put the pieces into a serving dish and arrange them so they look like something. Now you can put on each piece one of the thin corned beef slices. On 4 of these pieces put on a half egg, and one of the green olives you'll stick on with a toothpick. Now you'll put the broth in the pan you browned in and boil it together with the sherry for 1 minute. Scrape the pan while you're boiling so you'll mix in the little brown pieces in the broth. Pour this sauce over the veal and put the whole dish into a medium oven to warm up. Serve it right away, it shouldn't get cold. Serves 4 people. If it looks too good to eat, just close your eyes and start cutting.

* ALTE KAHKA: "that li'l ole winemaker, me!"

TANTE LEAH'S BRACIOLE CON CHIANTI*

2 steaks totalling 3 lbs.
A few pinches salt & pepper
Plenty of paprika
13 small or medium mush-
   rooms
6 small onions
A few thin slices pimiento
¼ cup finely rolled bread
   crumbs

½ cup melted parve marge-
   rine
1 tablespoon boiling water
1 whole raw egg
5 or 6 sliced stuffed olives
¼ cup parve margerine
½ cup flour
1 cup dry red wine

If you're friendly with your butcher, you'll get him to pound thin the steaks . . . if you're a little shy, you'll pound yourself at home. Rub in nice some salt, pepper, and plenty paprika. Put one steak a little bit over the long edge of the other one, so it looks like one large steak. Slice thin about 5 mushrooms and make a layer of them on the steaks. Next put a layer of very thinly sliced onion. Add small slices pimiento (you'll see as you work why everything has to be so thin). Cover all this with the bread crumbs. Now you'll beat together the melted margerine, boiling water, and raw egg . . . . and right away you should pour it over the bread crumbs. Place the olives in a row along one long edge of the steak, and begin to roll the meat. If you find you have too much stuff, take out a few things . . . . or maybe you didn't slice some things thin, like you were told. Tie the roll firmly with string. Sprinkle flour on the outside, and brown the roll in ¼ cup margerine. Put 8 mushrooms and 5 small onions in a large casserole dish and sprinkle more salt, pepper, and paprika on everything. Be sure to pour 1 cup of dry red wine in the dish. Cook this for about 2 hours in a 350° oven. Keep your eye on this and peep at it now and then . . . . and baste a little. If the liquid gets low, you'll add a little water. Serves 4 to 5 and is very good with rice, a big salad and garlic bread. Put some Italian music on the phonograph, turn the lights down low, fill the glasses with wine . . . . and you'll think you're in Italy. Drink enough of the wine, and you'll swear you're in Italy!

* CHIANTI: a favorite of the construction men who built the Tower of Pisa, which possibly accounts for its present state.

VEAL ROLLATINI ROMEO
AND JULIET*

½ lb. ground meat
1 nice beaten egg
1 clove garlic, chopped
½ teaspoon MSG
A few pinches salt
1 tablespoon parsley, chopped
1 teaspoon fennel
½ teaspoon anise seed
1 lb. thin veal cutlets
4 tablespoons olive oil

SAUCE:
1 chopped onion
2 chopped cloves garlic
A couple pinches basil
½ teaspoon oregano
A few pinches salt & pepper
1-6 oz. can tomato paste
1 cup tomato sauce
A little dash sherry
1 cup water

Mix together the ground meat, egg, garlic, MSG, salt, parsley, fennel and anise seed. Now the cutlets you'll cut into pieces 3-4 inches square and in the center of each piece put a little of the meat mixture. You can roll each cutlet like a *blintz* and stick in a toothpick so you shouldn't come apart. Put the olive oil into a skillet and brown the rolls all over. While they're browning, throw in the chopped onion and garlic, they should also brown. When this looks done, you can throw in the basil, oregano, salt, pepper, tomato paste, tomato sauce, sherry and water. Let this simmer with the cover on for 30 minutes and it's ready to serve with a nice Risotto to 4 hungry people, they should eat hearty!

* *ROMEO AND JULIET:* the famous play about the tragic love affair between Romeo Montague and Juliet Caplan, immortalized by William Shaeffer.

GEFILLTE BREAST OF VEAL
AHFTZZA LUCHAS*

1 - 4 lb. breast of veal with a pocket
½ cup parve oleo
1 onion, chopped
1 clove garlic, chopped
1 cup sliced mushrooms
3 cups bread crumbs
3 tablespoons parsley
A good pinch basil
A good pinch marjoram
1 teaspoon MSG
A little salt and pepper
2 fresh eggs, beaten
Enough water or broth to moisten
A big needle and strong thread so you can sew
A little flour
¼ cup water
¼ cup dry white wine
A little paprika

Sauté in ¼ cup oleo the onion, garlic and mushrooms. Meanwhile, mix together the bread crumbs with the parsley, basil, marjoram, MSG, salt, pepper and beaten eggs. Now you can throw in the onions, garlic and mushrooms. Mix this all together and add enough water or broth to make it nice and moist. You'll stuff the veal and then sew up the pocket with a needle and thread. Sprinkle good the veal with the flour and then brown it in the rest of the oleo in a large roasting pan on the top of the stove. Now add the water and wine, sprinkle the veal with a little paprika, put the cover on and roast it in the oven at 325° for 2 hours. If the weather is chilly, have yourself a small glass *schnapps* while this is cooking. If the weather is warm, drink it on the back porch. When the veal is done, mix in a little flour with the drippings and you'll see what a nice gravy it'll make. This will serve about 5 people or maybe 6, if you slice not too thick.

* *AHFTZZA LUCHAS:* when the maid who's been coming every week for 5 years quits the day before the *Bar Mitzvah*.

VEAL SCALOPPINE ALLA
VIA VENETO*

1½ lbs. veal steak
4 tablespoons flour
A few nice pinches salt
A pinch pepper

2 tablespoons parve margerine
¼ cup beef broth
2 tablespoons sherry
A few slices lemon

When you buy the veal, tell the butcher he should cut it nice and thin and pound it a little bit. Then, if he's not too busy, he can also cut it up in 4 inch pieces. If he's too busy, you'll cut it yourself. Then (when you get home, not in the butcher shop) you can mix all together the flour, salt and pepper and dip in it, the veal. Make sure you cover all over. Melt the margerine in a large frying pan and brown good the veal on both sides. When it's good and brown take it out from the pan and keep it warm. Next, you can pour in the pan the broth and the sherry. Cook this on a high fire and scrape up all the stuff from the bottom of the pan. Let it cook for about a minute and then you can pour it on the veal. Now put on the lemon slices. They look pretty on the dish and they're good to squeeze also. This will make plenty for 4 people. They should live and be well!

* *VIA VENETO:* Ocean Parkway with sidewalk cafes.

VEAL CHOPS GREPSELLA*

4 nice thick veal chops
1 cup wine vinegar
1 nice large egg
1 cup bread crumbs
¼ cup flour
1 tablespoon chopped parsley

1 teaspoon oregano
1 chopped clove garlic
A few pinches salt and
    pepper
4 tablespoons olive oil

First you'll soak the veal chops in the vinegar for about an hour. Then take them out from the vinegar and dry them good. Now beat up the egg with a little bit water and mix up good together the bread crumbs, parsley, oregano, garlic, salt and pepper. Cover good the chops in the flour, dip them a little in the egg and then with the bread crumbs you'll cover over. Now in a frying pan heat the oil and fry on both sides the chops 'til they're brown. Make a little lower the fire and cover the pan and let them cook for about 20 minutes so they'll be tender. This will serve 4 nibblers or 2 *hahzars*.

* *GREPSELLA:* the first thing out of your mouth after you drink the bi-carb.

LAMB STEW GEZUNTHEIT*

2½ lbs. lamb
2 tablespoons olive oil
1 large diced onion
2 pieces garlic, chopped
1 cup water
½ cup tomato sauce

1 teaspoon oregano
½ teaspoon mint leaves
A few good pinches salt
  & pepper
½ teaspoon MSG

Trim good the fat from the lamb and into 1½ inch cubes you should cut. Put the olive oil into a heavy pot and brown in it the pieces lamb. Then you can throw in the onions and they can also brown a little. Now add the rest of the ingredients, give it a stir, put on the cover and let it simmer for a half hour or so. When it's done, you can serve it to 4 or 5 people who'll practically be able to cut this with a fork. But maybe you should serve knives, just in case.

* *GEZUNTHEIT:* the thanks for this blessing is always said through a handkerchief.

SHMAGEGGI POT ROAST WITH WHITE WINE*

2 tablespoons olive oil
2 large onions, sliced
4 lbs. of chuck pot roast
1 cup of canned tomatoes
1 chopped up stalk celery

1 sliced carrot
1 cup of dry white wine
A few pinches each of salt,
pepper and basil

In the olive oil you'll fry the onions in a casserole dish until they're golden. Put in the beef, brown it good all over. Now add the vegetables, the white wine, the salt, pepper and basil. Put on the cover and simmer slowly for 3 hours. This is so delicious, you shouldn't know from it . . . and it'll serve 6 people. It's just a suggestion, but if you serve this with the *Broccoli Oy Ah Halairia* on page 72 and a rice dish, everybody'll ask you who catered the dinner.

* *SHMAGEGGI:* he thinks an audience with the Pope is both of them watching a movie together.

FOWL

CHICKEN CACCIATORE VINO ROSSO MOGEN DAVID*

1 large hen, 4 or 5 lbs.	1-6 oz. can tomato sauce
3 tablespoons olive oil	1-1 lb. can tomatoes
1 large onion, chopped	A pinch salt
3 cloves garlic, minced	A pinch pepper
1 rib celery, chopped	½ teaspoon oregano
1 cup sliced mushrooms	½ cup dry red wine

You'll be sure to cut up the chicken in serving pieces. Then heat the oil in a skillet and sauté the chicken until it's brown. Add the onion and garlic and push them around until they brown a little, too. Now you can add the celery, mushrooms, tomato sauce, tomatoes and the other seasoning. Cook very slowly for about an hour; and then, 5 minutes before you serve, you'll pour in the wine. When the whole thing's done, pour it over noodles or spaghetti and get back on the diet tomorrow! This takes good care of 4 or 5 people . . . if you serve lots of *forshpeisa*, you can maybe squeeze out for 6.

* *VINO ROSSO MOGEN DAVID:* a fancy name for Passover wine.

CHICKEN OREGANATE CON HUTZPAH*

½ cup flour
2 teaspoons oregano
1 tablespoon parsley flakes
2 teaspoons salt
½ teaspoon pepper

1-3 or 4 lb. chicken, cut up
¼ cup olive oil
1½ cup sliced mushrooms
½ cup dry white wine

Put in a clean paper bag the flour, oregano, parsley, salt and pepper. Put in 1 or 2 of the pieces chicken at a time, and give the bag some nice shakes. Don't go crazy with it or you'll find white clouds in the kitchen with chicken flying everywhere. Just shake so all the pieces are covered. Now you can put the olive oil in a large frying pan and brown the chicken all over. When they're browned golden you can put them in a baking dish. Don't throw away the oil, because now you'll put in it the mushrooms and sauté them until soft. Add the wine and scrape all the brown stuff off the bottom of the pan. Pour this on the chicken and put the whole thing into the oven for a half hour at 350°. If the pieces aren't done in a half hour—you'll just leave them a little longer; a few minutes more won't hurt. This will serve 4 or 5 people depending on how long they had to wait for dinner.

* HUTZPAH: what Molly had when, just because she went down to a size 18 dress, she bought a bikini.

CHICKEN ALLA NUDNIK*

A nice cut up 3 lb. fryer
½ cup flour
2 teaspoons salt
A little pinch pepper
¼ cup parve oleo

2 cups sliced mushrooms
1 cup chicken broth
1 tablespoon lemon juice
1 teaspoon grated lemon rind

Put the flour, salt and pepper in a paper bag and shake in it a few pieces chicken at a time until each piece is covered white all over. Now you'll heat up the oleo in a big enough casserole and brown in it the chicken on all sides. When the chicken is nice and golden, the mushrooms, chicken broth, lemon juice and rind you'll throw in. Cover the pot and let it simmer for a half hour until the chicken is done. Taste the sauce and if you think it needs, add a little more lemon juice. But don't get too sour—this isn't so good either. This will make plenty for 4-5 people and maybe tonight you'll skip yourself the dessert.

* NUDNIK: that persistent door-to-door salesman who couldn't understand why you wouldn't buy a New Testament.

CHICKEN NOODLES TZAZZKI*

1-3 lb. chicken
A few pinches salt
A few pinches pepper
2 tablespoons oil
3 large ribs celery, diced
4 green onions, chopped
1 medium onion, chopped
2 cloves garlic, minced
Some sprigs parsley, or
parsley flakes

1 can ripe olives (without
seeds), cut up in little
pieces
¼ cup cut up mushrooms
1 lb. noodles
1-6 oz. can tomato paste
1 tablespoon lemon juice
1 cup water (or ½ cup
water; ½ cup dry wine)

Boil the chicken in water with some salt & pepper so you'll have maybe a quart of stock. (Later the noodles you can boil in the stock.) The chicken has to cook until the meat is practically falling off the bones. When it cools down—if you hurry, you'll only burn yourself—take the meat from the bones. Sauté until they're tender the celery, onions, and garlic. Now put in the parsley, olives, mushrooms, salt and pepper.

Boil the noodles in the chicken stock until they're "al dente" .... this, by the Italians, means if the one who's cooking thinks the noodles are done, they're done. After the noodles have been drained, mix with them the chicken, tomato paste, lemon juice, water and wine, if you're using. Cook in a nice covered pot maybe 45 minutes on low heat ... and now and then, you'll stir. The whole thing serves 8-10 people. With a nice soup and salad, you don't have to serve anything else. ... and it's even better the next day.

* TZAZZKI: the "emerald" Moe bought in Naples that turned out to be cut from an old Chianti bottle.

68

VEGETABLES,

GAY IN DRAIRD STRING BEANS*

2 packages frozen "French style" string beans
1 nice onion, chopped
2 chopped pieces garlic
2 tablespoons olive oil
1 tomato, peeled and chopped
2 tablespoons chopped celery

2 tablespoons chopped parsley
1 teaspoon savory
A pinch basil
A couple pinches salt & pepper
2 tablespoons dry white wine

First you should prepare the string beans like the package says. While this is cooking, you can sauté the onion and garlic in the oil until it's a little brown. Then you can throw in the tomato, celery, parsley, savory, basil, and white wine and salt and pepper. Let this simmer good for 10 minutes and give it once in awhile a stir. When the string beans are done, drain from them the water and add them to the sauce that you've just simmered. Mix it all together and serve it good and hot. If you don't have savory on your spice shelf, buy some. It's the secret of the recipe. This has such an exotic flavor, you shouldn't ask! And it makes enough for maybe 8 people.

* *GAY IN DRAIRD:* what the Garfinkles said when that hotel in Palm Beach used the excuse "all booked up."

EGGPLANT PARMIGIANA LA DOLCE VITA*

1 cup olive oil
1 cup onions, chopped nice
2 pieces chopped up garlic
5 cups drained canned to-
matoes
1 tablespoon parsley
A few pinches salt to taste

A pinch pepper
2 nice large fresh eggs
2 tablespoons flour
2 medium eggplants
1 cup diced Mozzarella cheese
1 cup grated Parmesan cheese

Heat up in a frying pan 3 tablespoons oil and put in the onions and garlic until they're golden. Then you can throw in the tomatoes, parsley, salt and pepper and cook it for 25 or 30 minutes. Don't forget to give it once in a while a stir. While it's cooking you can cut up the eggplant into ½ inch slices and also mix together the eggs and flour into a batter. Now you'll dip each piece eggplant into the batter and fry them in the rest of the oil so they'll get good and brown. When they're all ready, put a layer eggplant into the bottom of a casserole, put on some sauce, then a little of the cheese and then some more eggplant. Keep doing this until you're all used up, and try to make the top layer cheese. If you pay attention to what you're doing, you won't have any trouble. Next you can put it into a moderate oven (350°) and let it bake for 25 to 30 minutes. This will make the cheese melt and make a mess from your casserole, but it's worth it. You should have enough for 5 or 6 people.

* LA DOLCE VITA: a hot pastrami, a sour pickle and thou be-side me in the Catskills.

❦ BROCCOLI OY AH HALAIRIA!*

1 bunch broccoli
A pinch salt
1 teaspoon anise seed

1 stick margerine
1 tablespoon lemon juice
1 teaspoon capers

First you'll clean good the broccoli and put it in a pot. Add an inch of water and the salt and the anise seed. Now you can steam it for 20 minutes. Meanwhile, you should melt the margerine and add the lemon juice and capers. When the broccoli is ready, put it in a nice serving dish, pour over the sauce and serve it to 4 people. Believe me, too many people just cook broccoli and serve it with nothing on it and it lies there like it's sad. This, we promise, will make happy broccoli.

* *OY AH HALAIRIA!*: street cleaner's lament after a festival on Mulberry Street.

BUPKAS BAKED CAULIFLOWER*

1 nice head cauliflower	½ cup chopped canned mush-rooms
2 tablespoons butter	
2 tablespoons flour	¼ cup bread crumbs
1 cup milk	1 tablespoon parsley, chopped
A few pinches salt	2 tablespoons Parmesan cheese
A pinch pepper	

Boil the whole cauliflower in salted water for 20 minutes. When it's ready, you'll break it up into small sections and put them into a baking dish. (Cauliflower looks so pretty when it's served in a red baking dish. If you have one, use it . . . . if not, don't run out and spend so easily.) Now melt the butter and mix in the flour until it's smooth. Pour in slow the milk and stir on a low fire until it gets thick. When this happens, you can throw in the mushrooms and parsley, together with the salt and pepper. Mix this all together and pour it over the cauliflower. On top of this, sprinkle the bread crumbs and then the grated cheese. Bake this at 375° for 20 minutes and serve to 4 skinny people who "need a little meat on their bones."

* *BUPKAS*: what you tipped the waiter in Milan who spilled Chianti on you.

73

STUFFED CABBAGE VIA SHMATAH*

1 large cabbage
2 onions, minced
1 lb. ground meat
2 tablespoons olive oil
1 cup cooked rice
1 teaspoon marjoram

1 teaspoon basil
2 tablespoons pine nuts (Pignoli)
1½ teaspoons salt
A dash pepper

FOR THE SAUCE YOU'LL USE:

1-6 oz. can tomato paste
½ cup water
¼ cup wine (dry red)
2¼ tablespoons brown sugar

¼ cup or a nice handful raisins
½ teaspoon salt
3 tablespoons lemon juice

Put the head cabbage in about 2 inches boiling water and leave about 8 minutes. After you drain it, you'll sauté the onions and you'll browhn the meat. This way you'll get rid of the extra fat in the meat. Now you'll mix the onions and meat with the rice, majoram, basil, nuts (if you found them at the grocery), and

1½ teaspoons salt, and pepper. Now put a leaf of the cabbage on the table and put about 3 heaping teaspoons mixture at the bottom of the leaf; you'll be able to tell better how much you'll need for each leaf. (Your cabbage may be bigger than my cabbage.) Fold the bottom of the leaf over once at the core end of the leaf. Fold both sides of the leaf toward the center and roll up. Just the way the roll is now, is the way it should be put in the pot (loose end down). If it makes you happier you can use toothpicks, but you don't really need them. Place the rolls in a casserole pot—a good size one.

For the sauce, you'll combine the tomato paste, water, wine, sugar, lemon juice, raisins and ½ teaspoon salt. Pour this over the cabbage rolls and turn on the television. (While the set's warming up, if you have any leftover veal or beef bones, throw them in, too.) Now you'll cover and simmer for 1-1½ hours, depending on how good the show is.

* VIA SHMATAH: a street in Rome where they sell second hand clothing.

MISHIGOYEM MUSHROOMS CON VINO BLANCO*

1 lb. small mushrooms	1 tablespoon parsley
3 tablespoons olive oil	2 cloves garlic, chopped fine
1 cup tomato sauce	Salt and pepper, to taste
1 cup dry white wine	

Put the mushrooms whole in a nice looking casserole. Pour in olive oil, tomato sauce, wine, parsley, garlic, salt and pepper. Now you'll give a few careful stirs to get everything mixed nice, cover, and put it in a 350° oven for about ½ hour. This dish you'll find very quick to make, and you'll like it. It serves maybe 4 people if they don't make *hahzars* of themselves.

* *MISHIGOYEM:* they think *Bar Mitzvah* is the name of an Israeli ranch.

76

DESSERT

SHIRLEY DE MEDICI'S RUM ICE CREAM*

4 egg yolks	1½ cups whipping cream,
4 tablespoons sugar	you'll whip
3 egg whites	¼ cup rum

Beat the egg yolks and sugar together long enough so they're nice and thick. (If you have an electric beater your arm won't be so tired.) In a separate bowl you'll beat stiff the egg whites. Now into the beaten yolks and sugar, fold the whites and whipped cream. After that's done, stir in the best part of all— the rum. Put it all in whatever fits nicely in your refrigerator and freeze it for at least 3 hours. This dessert serves 10 people; and if you're making it you better invite over 10 people or you'll be eating such calories all week and smell like you've been drinking rum all week!

---

* *SHIRLEY DE MEDICI:* (née Schwartz—'twas on the Isle of Capri that she met him.)

GELATIN CHEESE CAKE
NOSHEREI*

3-3 oz. boxes different colored
    Kosher gelatin
1 lb. Ricotta
1-3 oz. package cream cheese

½ cup candied fruits & peels
2 tablespoons sugar
1 teaspoon vanilla

Mix up each package gelatin separately like the box says. Now take a loaf pan (about 11 x 5 x 3), pour in the first color and let it set nice. Meanwhile, you'll mix up together the Ricotta, cream cheese, candied fruits and peels, sugar and vanilla. Now smear half of this on the first layer gelatin. Be careful to keep it at least a half inch away from all the sides so it shouldn't squish out later. Now pour on the next layer gelatin and let this set good. Put on the rest of the Ricotta mixture the same way and then the last layer gelatin. Chill this so everything gets nice and firm and when you're ready to serve, dip the pan in some hot water for a few seconds and then turn it quick upside down on a plate. Slice it up to serve as many people as you need for, (at least 12). If you use red and green gelatin, that with the white cheese filling and you'll have the colors of the Italian flag!

* NOSHEREI: this took the place of cigarettes when Nathan quit smoking. Now they call him "Fat Nat."

BOW-TIES CON AH TRINKELLA SCHNAPPS*

¼ lb. butter
3 egg yolks
2 whole eggs
1 tablespoon sugar
A little pinch salt
2 oz. whiskey

1 teaspoon vanilla extract
2 cups flour
A pot hot oil
A sprinkle can with pow-
   dered sugar

Cut first the butter into the egg yolks and eggs. Then add the sugar, salt, whiskey and vanilla. Now mix in the flour slowly and knead it a little bit. When this is done put it into the refrigerator for a half hour. While you're waiting and if the whiskey bottle is still out, pour yourself a little drink. A person that works in the kitchen as hard as you do deserves a glass *schnapps* once in a while. When the dough is through chilling, cut into 4 pieces and roll each piece on a floury board until its very thin. Then you can cut these pieces into strips 6 to 8 inches long and 1 inch wide. Take each piece and tie a little knot in it. You can fry them in the hot oil until they get a healthy golden color. Take them out from the oil and drain. Now sprinkle on the powdered sugar and they're ready to serve. Makes 25 to 30 pieces and they practically melt in your mouth!

* *AH TRINKELLA SCHNAPPS*: this is what made getting a cold fun when you were a kid.

ANISE COOKIES ZOL ZEIN
MIT GLICK*

3 cups flour
2 teaspoons baking powder
½ cup sugar
A pinch salt

½ cup parve margerine
2 fresh eggs
¼ cup milk
A handful anise seed

Mix together the flour, baking powder, sugar and salt. Now, if you're not so fussy, you'll mix in with your hands, the shortening. Then beat up the eggs and mix them in also. Pour in the milk and mix the whole sticky thing together until it looks smooth and forms a ball. Roll out the dough nice and thin and cut into cookies with a cookie cutter or the edge of a drinking glass. Sprinkle a little anise seed on each cookie and press the seeds in with your hand. The anise seed gives a little tiny taste of licorice. Now you can bake them on an ungreased baking pan in a 350° oven until they're browned a little, about 15 minutes. This will make 30 to 40 cookies, you and the kids will be nibbling for a week.

* ZOL ZEIN MIT GLICK: My goodness she's ugly! but you should both live and be well. . . .

CAFFE ESPRESSO SIGNORE DI HADASSAH*

To make good Italian coffee you need French roasted coffee. But you'll look first, you might find Italian roasted coffee at the grocery store in your neighborhood, or even in somebody else's neighborhood. Either one will do because they're both very black and ground very fine. If you want to get real fancy, you can buy an Italian *caffettiera*, which is an Italian coffee maker. . . . but the old drip coffee pot is O.K., too.

FOR OLD DRIP COFFEE POTS:

Boil 4 cups water.
Pour over 5 tablespoons coffee in the top of the pot, and let it drip.
Serve it in a little cup with a nice twist of lemon.
This makes about 8 small cups.

CAPPUCCINO

The experts say this you don't serve after a meal—only between meals and for breakfast. If it makes you feel better to serve it with bagel and lox, so serve! But it tastes just as good after a meal. So who needs rules?

For this you make like for the *espresso* only on top you put a tablespoon of hot cream or hot foamy milk or even whipped cream and a little sprinkle of cinnamon. The way this coffee gets its name is that it's supposed to be the color of the robes the Cappuccine monks wear. (Look—*everybody* can't be Jewish!)

* *CAFFE ESPRESSO:* what the ladies of Hadassah served with sponge cake to Marc Antony and his troops after the conquest of Egypt.

INDEX

THE FRENCH-KOSHER COOKBOOK

THE FRENCH-KOSHER COOKBOOK

 BY RUTH AND BOB GROSSMAN

To Todd Adam—
the new kid on the block

Thou shalt not eat any abominable thing . . .

And every beast that parteth the hoof, and cleaveth the cleft into two claws, and chewest the cud among beasts, that ye shall eat . . .

These ye shall eat of all that are in the waters: all that have fins and scales shall ye eat . . .

Of all clean birds ye shall eat . . .

But these are they of which ye shall not eat: the eagle, the ossifrage and the osprey . . . and the glede, and the kite, and the vulture after his kind,

And every raven after his kind . . .

And every creeping thing that flieth is unclean unto you: they shall not be eaten . . .

But of all clean fowls ye may eat . . .

Ye shall not eat of any thing that dieth of itself . . . thou shalt not seethe a kid in his mother's milk . . .

DEUTERONOMY XIV

PREFACE In most Kosher homes, there is a traditional culinary repertoire of dishes that are served with rather consistent regularity. And our homes were no exceptions. When Grandma, the *chef de cuisine* in Bob's home, found her grandchildren had become tired of the same limited dishes they had grown up with, she decided to do something about it to keep them coming over every week instead of wandering to greener, more delectable fields. So after coercing friends and family to assist her in gathering recipes of all nationalities, Grandma "took out from them the *hahzarye*," and made them as tasty as the originals—but Kosher. We thought perhaps others would enjoy Grandma's recipes in her inimitable language and compiled them in THE CHINESE-KOSHER COOKBOOK, which was followed shortly thereafter by THE ITALIAN-KOSHER COOKBOOK. Having conquered these two cuisines, Grandma inevitably turned to what many consider the finest cuisine in the world—French cooking. But this really frightened her . . . for she heard the French used all sorts of cream sauces on meats! ate

vii

all kinds of non-Kosher shellfish and parts of animals she never even heard of! She had never really eaten true French food, but this was not going to deter her. Grandma felt a trip to France could give her all the background she would need to be able to take the *trafe* out of French food and make it Kosher, yet authentic. But Grandma is eighty-three years old now and felt if she couldn't see all the gay spots of Paris and the museums and the famous landmarks—with maybe the Riviera thrown in—it really wouldn't be too much fun. And although she has lots of energy, Grandma had a better idea. She decided to send her grandchildren in her place . . . let us have all the fun, bring back the information, and then she could continue her seemingly endless job of making foods of all countries within the Dietary Laws. We had been to France before, but who could pass up such an offer! The reservations were made a year in advance so we could have a lovely ocean voyage aboard a truly French ship. New luggage was bought, a few new clothes purchased, spending money was saved . . . we read volumes of the latest tourist books on France . . . it was all we talked and thought about.

We never made that trip. And Grandma couldn't be happier. For now, in addition to our French poodle we have added a son, Todd Adam, to our family. And it looks like all our future recipes will have to read, "serves 4 or more." We never got to visit that synagogue in Lyon or the Hadassah group in Marseilles, but maybe next year . . .

Brooklyn Heights, N. Y.   Ruth & Bob Grossman

TABLE OF CONTENTS

THE FRENCH-KOSHER COOKBOOK

TRUFFLES SHMUFFLES!

From French food you can get heartburn, too. Like lots of other countries, France has its share of heavy food like BOEUF BOURGUIGNONE, which is really a beef stew with a fancy name. But nobody can make a nice delicate omelet or a CREPE SUZETTE (a fancy kind of blintz) like a Frenchman. Sometimes though, they surprise you with some of their *meshugenuh* food . . . calves' heads, frogs' legs, snails, woodcock with its own intestines yet, and even turtles. But in this book you'll find the kind of dishes you could bring home to Mother and she still wouldn't know what they were. But one thing sure—you'll know they're really French and they're guaranteed Kosher.

Before you start running to the stove, stop first and a little inventory you'll take in the kitchen. The French do most of their cooking in good heavy pots so the heat goes all over evenly, and it's pretty sure the foods won't stick and burn. Copper pots are nice to cook in and they look so *mench* sitting around a kitchen. . . . but if you don't have them, heavy enamel cast iron ones are wonderful. (Some of them are so heavy you could get a hernia, but such food you'll cook in them!) For your sauces you should have a big wire whisk. You could maybe live without one, but this looks very French in the kitchen. But what you can't live without is a good sieve so you can strain soups and sauces that need

1

straining, and they're good for puréeing vegetables and things. Your omelet pan shouldn't be just any pan you cook regular eggs in. It should be kept only for omelets. You never wash an omelet pan (the neighbors don't have to know . . . some things you should keep to yourself). You just wipe it clean with maybe a paper towel. This way it gets "seasoned" and your omelets never stick to it, because a stuck omelet becomes a scrambled egg.

All through this book you'll see, if you keep your eyes open, the words "bouquet garni". This has nothing to do with flowers. It's just a clean *shmatah* that holds lots of nice spices like sprigs of parsley, a little thyme, a bay leaf, peppercorns and sometimes a clove or two. You just tie a string around the bundle and let it sit in whatever you're cooking when the recipe says so and all those delicious flavors just cook in. Afterwards, you don't have to strain . . . just throw away the "bouquet garni".

You'll notice the French use a lot of wine in their cooking . . . but the alcohol cooks off, so don't worry about getting drunk. And when the recipe says a "dry" wine, don't use a sweet wine or everything will taste like dessert . . . there are plenty good Kosher dry wines.

Also, you'll see that some of these recipes call for different kinds cheeses. Again you shouldn't worry, there are plenty good Kosher cheeses.

Some people get shallots mixed up with scallions. But shallots are like a cross between onions and garlic and a scallion is a scallion. But if you can't get shallots, you can use the white parts of scallions. They're almost just as good.

Beurre manié is a wonderful way to make thick the juices in vegetables that some people throw out. To make it you knead together the same amount of butter and flour until it makes a soft ball. Then you break the ball into little pieces and drop it in the peas, beans or whatever you're binding together, and swirl it around until it's thickened. With a *fleishig* meal, you'll use *parve* oleo with the flour and it's just as good and a lot more Kosher.

Truffles are very popular in France and very expensive in America . . . so if you can afford to have truffles lying around the house, you'll throw away this book and hire your own French chef—but you'll make sure he's Kosher. Bon appétit!

2

HORS D'OEUVRES

PÂTÉ DE FOIE SCHMALTZ*

1 lb. chicken livers   ¼ teaspoon white pepper
1 nice sliced onion   1 teaspoon salt
5 tablespoons schmaltz   ¼ teaspoon savory
1 tablespoon sherry

Broil first the livers. While they're broiling, you can fry in the schmaltz until golden and soft, the onion. Now add a little of the broiled livers and a little of the onion into the blender and blend. Blend a small batch at a time until it's all done If you don't have a blender, chop up the whole works in a chopping bowl and then push it through a sieve. Now you can add the spices and the sherry, and mix yourself up good. Pour this into an ovenware bowl and cover it up tight. (If there's no cover, use foil.) Now stand this in a large pan with a few inches of water in it. Put the whole thing into a 400° oven and let it cook for 2 hours. Then you can chill and garnish with parsley and shredded carrots for a *forshpeis*, canape, or just plain *nosh*.

* *SCHMALTZ*: the Jewish answer to the 70¢ spread.

4

GEHAKTE PÂTÉ DE
SACRE BLEU!*

1 lb. chicken livers	½ cup dry red wine
2 lbs. ground meat	1 tablespoon flour
1 onion, chopped	½ teaspoon dry mustard
3 shallots, chopped	½ teaspoon white pepper
1 clove garlic, chopped	½ teaspoon ginger
1 tablespoon chicken schmaltz	1 teaspoon salt
3 tablespoons solid Kosher vegetable shortening	1 tablespoon parsley
2 nice eggs	1 teaspoon MSG

First, broil the livers to "kosher" them. While you're broiling, you can sauté the onion, shallots and garlic in the schmaltz and shortening. When this is all done, mix it, schmaltz and all, together with the eggs, wine, flour and spices. Now you can purée this with the chicken livers in a blender, if you have. If you don't have, then chop up the livers nice and fine and mash them together with the other stuff. Now you'll mix up with the chopped meat and put the whole thing into a meat loaf pan and with foil you'll cover it. Put this pan into a bigger pan that has about an inch of water in it. Then the whole thing you can put into a 300° oven for 2 hours. For the last 20 minutes the foil you should take off. When it's all done, chill for at least 8 hours. After it's chilled, you'll dip the pan into hot water for 15 seconds. This will loosen it a little. Turn it upside down on a serving plate. If you dipped long enough it'll plop right out. Decorate the top a little with parsley or chopped hard-boiled egg . . . don't *umgepatch* too much. Now you'll slice it thin for a *forshpeis*, or if you're a real "big shot"—you'll have an hors d'oeuvre.

SACRE BLEU!: the French answer to *Oy Gevalt!*

KNISH LORRAINE*

FIRST, THE PASTRY SHELLS YOU'LL MAKE:

2 cups flour

⅔ cup Kosher vegetable shortening

¾ teaspoon salt

7 tablespoons cold water

Sift good together the flour and the salt and then with 2 knives or with a pastry blender you'll cut in good the shortening until the pieces are like the size of grains of rice. Now, sprinkle on 1 tablespoon of water and mix it up with a fork. Then add the next tablespoon of water and mix, and you'll just keep doing this until all the water has been used and the dough is moist. Now take it out from the bowl in your hand, and press it together into a ball. (Don't be afraid. You can wash later your hands.) The ball you'll sit in the refrigerator for a few minutes. Then take it out and roll it on a floured table till it's a big sheet of dough about ⅛ inch thick. Cut the dough into 5 inch circles. For this you'll use a bowl or anything you've got lying around that's about that size. These circles of dough you'll mold nicely over an upside down muffin tin, and bake them in a 450° oven for 15 minutes. (Remember the muffin tin is upside down . . . it's no mistake.) When they're done, you'll take them off carefully from the muffin tins and all of a sudden, little cups you've got! Whatever you do, don't make any holes in the dough, or later everything will run out from the shells and will your face be red! This makes about 12 shells. If you're not exactly 12, that's all right too.

6

NOW, THE FILLING WE'LL MAKE:

1 thinly sliced onion
2 teaspoons butter
4 lightly beaten eggs
1 cup cream

½ cup milk
½ teaspoon salt
A good pinch pepper
½ cup diced Swiss cheese

¼ cup Parmesan cheese, grated

First, you'll sauté the sliced onion in the butter until it's nice and soft. Meanwhile, together mix the eggs, cream, milk, salt and pepper. You'll put in each shell a few pieces of the sliced onion and on top of that put a little Swiss cheese. Now into each shell pour some of the egg-cream mixture. You'll put the same amount in each shell. On top of each, sprinkle the Parmesan cheese. Now very carefully put the shells on a cookie sheet or anything big and flat and put them in a 450° oven for about 25 minutes. Serve them right away, they're delicious hot. This, to tell you the truth, is not really a Knish; but then it's no Lorraine either. You try to put a filling like this in a real Knish and see what'll you'll get. Serves 12 delicate friends . . . or 6 adventurers who like everything in two's.

*KNISH: a New York politician could never be elected without eating one.

AVOCADO VINAIGRETTE
GAY AVEC*

FOR THE VINAIGRETTE SAUCE, YOU'LL HAVE:

½ cup oil
¼ cup wine vinegar
A good pinch salt
An also good pinch black pepper

1 tablespoon chopped chives
1 tablespoon chopped parsley
2 nice size cloves garlic,
   chopped fine

½ teaspoon paprika

This is so simple to do, it's almost embarrassing. All you do is mix together everything, put it in a jar, and you'll give a nice shake.

NOW, THE MOST IMPORTANT THING OF ALL:

3 ripe avocados
A little shredded lettuce

With a sharp knife cut each avocado in half the long way around. Pull apart nice and easy, and take from the middle the big round pit. On each salad plate, you'll put some shredded lettuce, then a half of avocado, then you pour in the hole enough VINAIGRETTE SAUCE to almost fill the hole. If you should have any of the sauce left over, it makes a nice dressing for regular salads. This will serve 6 people who, believe me, had better like avocados or they'll just be out of luck.

*GAY AVEC: the new advertising slogan of Pierre Shapiro's Travel Bureau.

GEFILLTE FISH REMOULADE*

In France the Remoulade Sauce they make is like Tartar Sauce they make here. But in New Orleans, the French chefs make a Remoulade Sauce that's a Remoulade Sauce! This is how they do it:

2 tablespoons lemon juice	1 tablespoon parsley
2 tablespoons tarragon vinegar	A pinch black pepper
	1 teaspoon paprika
2 tablespoons prepared mustard	A good sprinkle cayenne pepper
	1 cup vegetable oil
2 tablespoons horseradish	¼ cup fine chopped celery
A good pinch salt	¼ cup fine chopped scallions

Mix together good the lemon juice, vinegar and the rest of the spices. Then throw in the oil, celery and scallions. This you'll blend together good with a beater, or even a blender.

FOR THE REST YOU'LL NEED:

1-1 lb. jar gefillte fish balls   Shredded lettuce, to serve on

Arrange nice the balls on some shredded lettuce and a little sauce you'll pour on. One thing you shouldn't forget, serve this good and cold. This should be enough for 4 or even 5 people. If you're not serving so many, you can put the rest of the sauce in the refrigerator for next time. It keeps for 120 years, it should live and be well.

*GEFILLTE FISH: a popular *forshpeis* in Catholic homes on Friday night.

9

FAHBISSENAH EGGS EN GELÉE*

FIRST, YOU'LL MAKE AN ASPIC WHICH, IF YOU DON'T LIKE, YOU'LL FORGET ABOUT THIS RECIPE:

1½ cups chicken broth
½ cup tomato juice
2 envelopes unflavored Kosher gelatin
½ teaspoon sugar

1 crushed eggshell
1 beaten egg white
Salt & pepper, it should taste
1 tablespoon cognac

Heat the chicken broth, tomato juice, gelatin, sugar, eggshells and whites, and salt and pepper all together. Pull up a chair, because you have to stir it constantly and you'll remove it from the heat when the whole thing boils up like a froth. Stir in the cognac (if you haven't finished it in the excitement) and then strain this mish-mash through a cloth, you'll make sure it's clean. Spoon about 3 tablespoons of the aspic into each of 4 custard cups you should have somewhere in the house. Put the cups in the refrigerator and leave them there until they get nice and firm.

NOW COMES THE REST OF IT:

4 eggs
4 thin slices of corned beef, about the size of the poached eggs

Poach the eggs and let them cool themselves on a plate. Take out from the refrigerator the custard cups and put in the cups a cooled egg in each one . . . and on top of that you'll put a slice of the corned beef. Pour now the rest of the aspic divided nice and even into the custard cups and back into the refrigerator to chill. When it's time to unmold, and don't rush it (be sure it's nice and firm), dip each cup into a bowl of warm water and quick turn the cups upside down on individual serving plates. This *forshpeis* is so nice and delicate everybody will still have room for the rest of the meal and not get the cholesterol count pushed up too much. You can make it ahead of time so you'll be able to have a nice cocktail with your 3 guests, if you didn't sneak too much cognac from the aspic.

*FAHBISSENAH: if his smile was his umbrella, he'd get drenched!

10

SOUPS

L'OIGNON SOUP LEVINE
AND ROSE*

5 onions, thinly sliced
4 tablespoons oleo
7 cups vegetable bouillon
1 teaspoon sugar

1 cup dry white wine
Salt & pepper to taste
6 pieces crusty French bread
½ cup grated cheese

Sauté the onions in the oleo, they should be soft. Then you'll pour in the vegetable bouillon, the sugar and the wine and give a healthy stir. Put on the cover and you'll simmer for an hour. Then you'll put in the salt and pepper and taste it to see if it's enough. Don't overdo it; but on the other hand, onion soup has got to have a real taste. Put in each deep bowl one slice bread and over it you'll sprinkle with a lot of generosity the grated cheese. Pour the soup now over the bread in the bowl and eat hearty! This is a man-sized soup for 6 people or if you have dainty lady-size bowls, maybe you'll squeeze out a few more portions. Just be sure you have enough bread cut or you'll have hurt feelings, which don't mix well with onion soup.

*LEVINE AND ROSE: a French tune popular throughout the world.

12

QUEL DOMMAGE POTAGE DE PETITS POIS*

3½ cups shelled peas   1 teaspoon sugar
½ cup heavy cream   Salt & pepper to taste

Cook the peas in a half cup water with the sugar added, until
they are nice and tender. Next you'll drain them and purée
the peas with the cream in a blender, or a sieve if you never
got around to buying that blender. Add enough salt and pepper
so it should taste like something, and warm the soup . . . don't
boil it or only you will be responsible . . . until it's comfortable
enough to eat. This soup will have such a beautiful avocado
color, you shouldn't know from it! And it will be very fattening
for 4 skinny people. You can use canned peas for this dish—
but somehow, that seems like cheating. But look—it's your
business what you do in your kitchen. You do like your con-
science says.

*QUEL DOMMAGE: when you write a check to the *shul* for a
big donation and it bounces.

VEGETABLE SOUP SANS
PIÈCE DE RÉSISTANCE*

2 sliced onions	2 sliced carrots
2 stalks celery	A little salt, you should taste
2 tablespoons parve oleo	A couple dashes pepper
4 cups vegetable bouillon	A pinch marjoram
2 medium sliced potatoes	1 teaspoon MSG

2 tablespoons chopped parsley

Sauté nice the onions and celery in the oleo. In a pot you'll put the vegetable bouillon, the sautéed onions and celery, and also the raw potatoes and carrots. Cook this whole thing on a low fire until everything is soft. When this is done, purée everything through a sieve or put it in a blender until it's all nice and smooth. Put in now your seasonings—and don't be shy . . . nobody likes food that tastes like nothing. Simmer maybe 5 minutes more and you'll have a soup that'll bring smiles to 4 vegetarians.

* PIÈCE DE RÉSISTANCE: those little yellow eggs in the chicken soup Grandma gave you when you were good.

VICHYSSOISE DE MADAME POMPADOUR*

6 medium onions, sliced
5 medium potatoes,
  peeled & sliced thin
6 cups vegetable bouillon
3 cups milk

1 cup cream
1 teaspoon salt
½ teaspoon white pepper
2 teaspoons Worcestershire Sauce
¼ cup chopped chives

Mix the sliced onions together with the potatoes and the vegetable bouillon and cook it over a low heat for 45 minutes so the flavors get mixed up all nice and delicious. When it's done, push the whole thing through a sieve, it should be very fine. Stir in now the milk, cream, salt, pepper and Worcestershire Sauce. On top, sprinkle the chives and when it's cooled down a bit, put it into the refrigerator and let it get good and cold. Even though this is a heavy soup, for warm weather it's wonderful because it's cold. This may look like an anemic borsht, but it's a healthy soup for 8 run-down people.

*MADAME POMPADOUR: the famous *shiksa* with the famous *shaytel*.

BORSHT A L'ENFANT TERRIBLE*

8-10 medium beets	Salt & pepper, it should taste
6 cups water	2 tablespoons lemon juice
1½ cups dry red wine	2-3 tablespoons sugar
2 eggs beaten up nice	

Wash and peel the beets nice and carefully. Next you'll grate the beets, but be careful you shouldn't grate your fingers too and make from the soup a big mess. In a large pot you'll put now the grated beets together with the water and wine. Add the salt and pepper and taste to be sure everybody else will be able to taste, too. Let the whole thing simmer for a half hour. Add now the lemon juice and the sugar, give a stir, and give another taste to be sure the borsht will be "sweet and sour-y" enough.

Take the pot from the fire and let it cool uncovered. Stir in the beaten up nice eggs and the soup's finished. You can serve it hot or you can put in the refrigerator and let it get nice and cold. Don't forget to serve with it a big tablespoon of sour cream in each bowl. This will make enough for 6 to 8 people who only *thought* they'd had good borsht before.

*L'ENFANT TERRIBLE: the kid next door who taught all the boys on the block how to smoke.

16

SALADS & DRESSINGS

NAOMI'S NIÇOISE SALAD*

2 cups cooked French style
   string beans
2 cups cooked diced potatoes
10 rolled anchovies

Several thin strips pimiento
½ cup pitted black olives
1 cup VINAIGRETTE SAUCE,
   see p. 8

Mix together good the string beans and potatoes with the VINAIGRETTE SAUCE. Make one big heaping mound of this mixture on a serving plate. Now you'll decorate this mound with the anchovies, pimiento strips and olives. Some people even like hard-boiled egg slices and tomato wedges to decorate with. This is also good, but not an absolute must. This fancy salad serves 4 fancy people and is especially popular with people who usually can't stand salads.

*NAOMI: that poor girl in the Bible whose mother-in-law Ruth was always *shlepping* along after her.

FAH TUHMULD TONGUE SALAD*

½ lb. cooked tongue
3 tablespoons oil
1 tablespoon wine vinegar
1 tablespoon chopped onions

1 tablespoon chopped chives
2 tablespoons chopped parsley
A little salt & pepper
Some lettuce to serve on

Slice thin the tongue into little strips. Mix together the oil, vinegar, onions, chives, parsley, salt and pepper and pour this whole thing over the tongue strips. Put the mixture on a bed of lettuce and serve it to 3 or 4 people maybe with a cool lemonade. This makes a good salad, hors d'oeuvre, or a nice hot-weather lunch. Anyhow, it's a good way to use leftover tongue. You might have to buy sliced tongue at a delicatessen, because cooked leftover tongue you won't find at the butcher.

*FAH TUHMULD: what happened when Miriam told her folks she had the lead in the school Christmas play.

SHADKEN SALADE À
LA RUSSE*

1 cup of diced cooked potatoes	½ cup chopped celery
1 cup of diced cooked chicken, leftover is nice	½ cup chopped beets, cooked
½ cup cooked green peas, drained	½ cup chopped apples
	Salt & pepper, a few pinches
	2 hard-boiled eggs
	1 cup mayonnaise

You'll remember first, this is a cold salad, so all those things that have to be cooked can be leftovers or cooked earlier and then made cold in the refrigerator. Then you'll mix everything together (except the eggs) with the mayonnaise. (If you have the time, you shouldn't miss making the mayonnaise that's on p. 54.) Pile it up nice in a serving dish and with the slices of hard-boiled egg, you'll decorate. With this salad, you can be so creative and mix all kinds things together if you don't have all these ingredients. Not even a Russian would know the difference! This'll serve 6 to 8 people depending on how much *hahzarye* you threw into the salad.

*SHADKEN: she's lobbying to get Sadie Hawkin's Day made a national holiday.

GREEN SHMENDRICK SALAD
AVEC DRESSING FRANÇAISE*

FOR THE DRESSING, YOU'LL NEED:

1 teaspoon altogether of parsley,   3 tablespoons oil
chives, chervil & tarragon   ¼ teaspoon prepared mustard
1 tablespoon vinegar

Mix everything together so all the flavors blend and you'll
have *some* dressing!

FOR THE SALAD, YOU'LL NEED:

Lettuce   Escarole
Romaine   1 clove garlic
Chicory

You can use any or maybe all of the greens listed here and
you'll wash them very carefully—who knows what kind of non-
sense they sprayed on them!—and dry them very carefully.
The French put the leaves in a little basket and shake them
dry (you can use a paper towel) because they say the water
will make the dressing weak. So you don't take any chances,
dry already.

Rub with the clove garlic, the salad bowl—a wooden one is
nice—put in the mixed greens, pour in the dressing and mix
together like a real chef so all the leaves, they'll be coated. In
France, this is the salad that seems to be everybody's favorite
to eat with a meal . . . 400,000 Frenchmen can't be wrong,
especially if they're all Jewish.

*GREEN SHMENDRICK: a popular radio character who had a
Philippine houseboy named Mendel.

21

EGG
&
MATZOH DISHES

TROMBENIK OMELET
AUX TRUFFES*

2 tablespoons chopped truffles	2 tablespoons milk
3 tablespoons butter	1 tablespoon brandy
6 nice fresh eggs	Salt & pepper to taste

Truffles are very special and very popular in France. In America, you'll buy them in certain stores in little cans, they're not cheap. You'll cook them nice in the butter in your favorite omelet pan—it should be a large one (11 inches across) with not very high sides. In the meantime, you can mix up the eggs with the milk, brandy, salt and pepper. Take out from the pan the truffles and mix them in with the egg mixture. Pour the whole thing back into the omelet pan and cook on a medium fire until it sets nice. While it's setting, with a fork you'll lift the egg very little from the pan here and there and tilt the pan slightly, so the liquid mixture can run underneath. Keep doing this all around the pan the whole time it's cooking. It's not so complicated as it sounds. When the omelet looks like it's done, it probably is. Slide it out from the pan onto a plate and fold it in half, you'll be careful and don't rush. Cut it into serving portions—you can probably feed 2 or 3 people with it. A slice or two of toast . . . some nice fresh coffee . . . and you've got a real *mench* breakfast.

*TROMBENIK: if he did half the things he claims he did, there'd be two of him!

EGGS BENEDICT SANS
HAHZARYE*

8 nice fresh eggs
8 thin slices baloney
8 slices toast with crust removed,
   you should be fancy
Parve HAYMISHA HOLLANDAISE SAUCE, see p. 30

First, you'll poach nice the eggs in a little salted water. While you're poaching, trim each slice baloney so it should be the same size as each piece toast. Now put one slice of baloney on each slice toast. Drain the poached eggs and put one on each slice baloney-covered toast. On top this whole thing you'll spoon a little HOLLANDAISE SAUCE, and keep spooning until it's all used up. Some people like this sauce so much . . . when they're finished with the eggs, they might ask for extra toast to wipe up the sauce. Maybe it's not what Amy Vanderbilt would do, but good is good . . . they should live and be healthy! This serves 8 light eaters or 4 who can put it away nicely.

*HAHZARYE: that greasy pig stuff!

24

SCRAMBLED OEUFS GRAND'MÈRE*

2 slices white bread,
    cut in ¼ inch cubes
3 tablespoons butter
8 nice fresh eggs

2 tablespoons milk
A pinch salt
A pinch pepper

Fry the bread cubes in the butter until they're crisp and brown and very appetizing looking. Now beat the eggs—but you'll beat lightly—with the milk, salt and pepper. Pour this into a pan you should butter generously, and make a medium fire under the pan. Stir the eggs and keep stirring until they're smooth and creamy and then put in the fried bread cubes. Mix them in nice with the eggs and it's ready to serve 4 hungry grandmothers, they should live and be well!

* *GRAND'MÈRE:* a *bubba* who has wine and cheese by the Seine instead of tea and cake on the stoop.

MESHUGENUH MUMZER
MATZOH BREI MORNAY*

FIRST, YOU'LL MAKE THE BREI:

4 matzohs   A good pinch salt & pepper
4 nice fresh eggs

Soak first the matzohs in some water so they'll get soft. Then you'll drain and mix in with the eggs, salt and pepper. Into a greased baking dish you can put this mish-mash and cook it in a 325° oven for 30 minutes. It'll rise a little bit and be much prettier than if you fried the matzohs—and you probably eat too much fried food anyway.

NOW, YOU'LL MAKE THE MORNAY SAUCE:

2 tablespoons butter   2 tablespoons Gruyère cheese, grated
2 tablespoons flour   ¼ teaspoon salt
1 cup of milk   A little black pepper

Melt the butter first in a saucepan on a low fire, and then stir in the flour, it should be smooth. Don't go anywhere; just stand there and keep stirring a little. Now you'll pour in slowly the milk (you're still stirring until it gets thick) and let it cook about 2 minutes more. Add now the cheese, salt and pepper —mix in good and *schoen!* a MORNAY SAUCE you have. This is a classic French sauce and you can use it over eggs, vegetables, and fish. But I'll give a penny for every French housewife who's ever used it with *Matzoh Brei*. . . .

When the *Matzoh Brei* is ready, you'll take it from the oven and cut it in wedges like you cut a pie. Spoon on a little sauce on top and you have nice Sunday brunch for 4 to 5 people. It tastes delicious with hot QUELLE HEURE-EST IL CAFÉ AU LAIT, see page 80.

*MESHUGENUH MUMZER: Abdel Nasser's Jewish name.

SAUCES

SAUCE BÉCHAMEL DE BRIGHTON BEACH*

2 tablespoons butter
1 tablespoon minced onion
2 tablespoons flour

A little pinch salt & pepper
1 cup hot milk

Melt in a saucepan the butter and cook in it the onion until it's nice and soft. Then you'll throw in the flour, stir it a little and cook a minute or two more, but don't let it get brown. Now you'll add slowly salt and pepper and pour in slowly the milk, it shouldn't get lumpy. Keep stirring all the time. (With these French sauces, when they say stir, it means you'll forget everything else and stir.) Cook this on a low fire and stir constantly until it gets nice and thick. After that you sit down and take a breath and just give a stir now and then and you'll be sure that fire is nice and low. Let this sauce cook gently for about 20 minutes, strain out the onion, and serve the sauce on eggs, vegetables, and fish.

The nice thing about this sauce is that if you add a little grated cheese to it, you'll have a nice CHEESE SAUCE; if you add a little sweet cream to it, you'll have a CREAM SAUCE; when you add a touch of curry, it'll make a tasty CURRY SAUCE; some prepared mustard stirred in makes a MUSTARD SAUCE, etc. And it's right every time.

This, by the French, is one of their most important sauces. When you know how to make it, you'll be like a *mayvin* of sauces and you'll probably get all kinds invitations to cater Bar Mitzvahs and sweet sixteen parties, you should live so long!

*BRIGHTON BEACH: the Jewish Riviera.

28

SHMOOZING SAUCE BRUN*

2 cups vegetable stock
Salt & pepper, for a real flavor
1 teaspoon MSG
1 bouquet garni (2 sprigs parsley,
½ small bay leaf & a pinch
thyme all tied in a little piece
cloth)

4 tablespoons *parve* oleo
5 tablespoons flour

First, in a saucepan you'll simmer the stock with the salt, pepper, MSG, and the bouquet garni for maybe 20 minutes. Meantime, in another pan you'll melt the oleo and stir in the flour. Keep stirring until the flour turns into a nice nutty brown—believe me, this is the nicest kind of brown. Take out from the stock the *shmatah* of bouquet garni and pour the stock slowly into the browned flour. You'll be sure to keep stirring, you shouldn't get lumpy. Let the sauce boil till it's thick, then boil 3 minutes more—all the time you're stirring. This is a good sauce to know about. If you add sautéed mushrooms, you'll have a delicious MUSHROOM SAUCE. When you add a little dry red wine, you'll have—what else!—WINE SAUCE. By adding several teaspoons of horseradish, you have an unusual HORSERADISH SAUCE and it goes on and on. The French are nice and smart that way. This sauce makes 2 cups and it's very good poured on meat and anything else you feel like pouring on.

*SHMOOZING: the principle factor in the spectacular growth of AT&T.

HAYMISHA HOLLANDAISE SAUCE*

YOU SHOULD NOTE:

(For *fleischig* meals use *parve* oleo instead of butter)

4 large egg yolks	1 tablespoon lemon juice
½ lb. melted sweet butter	A little pinch salt
1 tablespoon cold water	A sprinkle cayenne pepper

Beat very good the egg yolks in the top of a double boiler and make sure the bottom has hot, but not boiling, water. When the yolks are a nice lemon color and thickened, you'll add *very* slowly, drop by drop (there's no reason to hurry) the melted butter and you'll keep stirring. Even if the phone rings, you'll keep stirring. Soon it'll start to thicken a little like mayonnaise. Dribble in the rest of the butter very slowly and remember, you're still stirring. Add next the lemon juice, salt and pepper. Stir it in a little and it's done. Be careful it doesn't get too hot or, believe me, you won't have Hollandaise Sauce, you'll have scrambled eggs which would look pretty silly sitting on top vegetables, fish or even poached eggs.

HAYMISHA: that nice politician who, when he came to your neighborhood, ate *knishes* and kissed the baby.

30

BAR MITZVAH BÉARNAISE
SAUCE*

2 tablespoons tarragon vinegar   ½ cup melted *parve* oleo
¼ cup dry white wine   A small dash cayenne pepper
2 shallots, chopped   A little salt
3 egg yolks   ½ teaspoon chopped chervil
A little chopped parsley

First, you'll put the vinegar, wine and shallots in a saucepan and let this boil until half of it is cooked away. Now you'll turn off the fire and put the wine and vinegar mixture aside and start working with a double boiler that has hot, but not boiling, water in the bottom. In this you'll beat good the egg yolks until they're thickened. Then add the melted oleo *very* slowly and you'll stir all the time, until the sauce is nice and thick and the oleo is all poured in. Mix in the wine and vinegar mixture, the pepper, salt, chervil and parsley, and you have now a sauce that's wonderful to serve on steaks and chops. Some people don't think you should put anything on steaks; but, believe me, some of the steaks some people have the nerve to serve should be rescued with a good sauce. BÉARNAISE SAUCE is delicious on all kinds steaks—good and bad.

*BAR MITZVAH: separates the men from the boys.

MEATS

FILET MINYAN WITH
MUSHROOM SAUCE*

YOU'LL NEED FIRST:

4 nice thick rib steaks

Take the rib steaks and cut out from the middle of each one the round meaty part. The bones and other things you'll give to the dog or you'll save for a nice soup. Broil these steaks to however you like them. While you're broiling,

YOU'LL FIX NOW THE MUSHROOM SAUCE:

3 tablespoons *parve* oleo
3 tablespoons flour
1 cup beef broth

½ cup dry red wine
A little salt & pepper
1½ cups sliced mushrooms

Cook the flour in 2 tablespoons of oleo, until it's nice and brown. Then you can slowly pour in the beef broth, all the time stirring. Now you'll add the wine, salt and pepper. Let this whole thing simmer uncovered for 15 minutes. Sauté the mushrooms in the rest of the oleo for a few minutes, they should be soft. Mix this in good with the sauce, keep it warm and when the steaks are done, you'll pour over each steak and they're ready to serve 4 Kosher gourmets, they should live to be 120 and still have a hearty appetite.

*MINYAN: when this is needed, no boy over 13 is safe in front of a *shul.*

OYS GEHMAHTET DAUBE GLACE*

3-4 lbs. lean roast
2 tablespoons oil
1½ cups rich beef stock
2 large onions, quartered
1 bay leaf
A pinch thyme
2 cloves garlic, sliced

Salt & black pepper, to taste
Cayenne pepper, to taste
2 ozs. sherry
2 cups water
2 packages unflavored Kosher
gelatin

Rub the meat nice with salt and pepper and then brown it in a little oil in a big pot. Then add the beef stock to the pot along with the onions, bay leaf, thyme, garlic, salt, black pepper and cayenne pepper. Now you'll take it easy for about 3 hours while the meat simmers till it's nice and tender. Every now and then, you can stroll into the kitchen and give a little stir to be sure there's still liquid in the pot. You don't have to, but there's something wrong with you if that smell of roast doesn't call you in. When the meat's done, you'll take it from the pot and strain the stock. Now put the stock back into the pot, add the sherry, 2 cups water and boil. From the fire you'll remove. Now add the gelatin (which you just made soft in a little water) and be sure to skim off the fat from the stock. Take a mold and put the meat in it. You decide what kind of mold. It doesn't matter, as long as it's deeper than the meat. Pour over the meat the stock, till the meat is covered. You might skim a little more. Then put the mold in the refrigerator and leave overnight. When it's set, you'll dip the mold in hot water for a few seconds, then turn it upside down on a platter, and so! Decorate here and there with some parsley sprigs, tomato wedges, green pepper rings, curly carrot slices, etc.

This kind of cold dish you see maybe at weddings and *Bar Mitzvahs* . . . so the family will call you a regular chef when they see this on the table. But then, too, they might say, "So what are we having hot tonight?" Serves about 6 complainers.

OYS GEHMAHTET: how Debbie felt after picketing all day at the Jordan Pavilion at the World's Fair.

BOEUF BOURGUIGNON
DE ROTHSCHILD*

2½ lbs. nice lean beef, cubed
Flour to dust
Salt & pepper, it should have
  a taste
5 tablespoons *parve* oleo
1 large chopped onion
2 cloves garlic, chopped fine

1 chopped carrot
3½ cups dry red wine
1 tablespoon parsley, chopped
1 bay leaf
A good pinch thyme
½ lb. sliced mushrooms
10 small onions

Dust very good the beef with the flour, salt and pepper. Melt 3 tablespoons oleo in a big casserole pot and then throw in the floured meat chunks and brown them a golden color on all sides. While you're browning, you can also throw in the chopped onions, garlic and carrot and push them around a little. When everything is browned nice, pour off the extra fat —be careful you don't pour out your ingredients, too. Next you'll pour in the wine and add the parsley, bay leaf and thyme. Put on the cover and cook in a 350° oven for about 1½ hours. Before you get too comfortable in some other room, you'll sauté first the mushrooms in 1 tablespoon oleo and when that's done, take out from the pan the mushrooms and put aside. Now in the same pan you'll melt the last tablespoon oleo and brown good the small onions whole. Put the onions with the mushrooms and, if your kitchen's not too ventilated, go watch television. After the 1½ hours in the oven, throw in the mushrooms and small onions in the casserole pot and cook covered for another 30 minutes. When it's all done, you should have enough Boeuf for about 6 people who, if they'll call this "stew," you have permission to throw this book at them.

*DE ROTHSCHILD: the nice Jewish family everyone was so friendly with when they moved to town.

FLEMISH CARBONNADES À VOTRE SANTÉ*

2 lbs. chuck cut into 1 inch
squares
⅓ cup flour
4 tablespoons oil
3 nice onions, sliced
2 tablespoons tomato paste

1–12 oz. can beer
2 teaspoons MSG
1 tablespoon parsley
1 bay leaf
½ teaspoon thyme
A few pinches salt & pepper

Dust nice the meat with the flour. Now put the oil into a big pot and cook a little the onions. When they're done, take them out from the oil and put in the pieces meat so they should brown. Now put back into the pot the onions and then the rest of the stuff. Put on the pot the cover, and cook the whole thing on a low fire for 2 hours or, if the butcher sold you tough meat, until it's tender. Don't worry about the beer. For this you don't have to "acquire maybe a taste." It's hidden nice and the whole dish will give 4 to 6 people a hearty appetite.

*À VOTRE SANTÉ: the difference between a continental and a drunk.

36

VEAL CUTLETS CHERCHEZ LA FEMME WITH CHIVES*

1½ lbs. veal cutlets	1½ cups beef or vegetable stock
⅓ cup flour	1 tablespoon flour
A few pinches salt & pepper	½ teaspoon thyme
4 tablespoons *parve* oleo	2 tablespoons sherry
1 tablespoon chopped chives	

Pound good the cutlets so they're nice and thin. Mix up the salt and pepper with the ⅓ cup flour and dust with this the cutlets. Now put the oleo into a nice size skillet and brown on both sides the cutlets. When they're good and brown, take them out from the pan and put in the stock and 1 tablespoon flour. Now you'll stir good so there shouldn't be lumps. Throw in next the thyme and sherry and scrape from the pan all the little bits of brown stuff. Put the cutlets back in the pan. Put on the cover and you'll simmer for 20 minutes. The last 2 minutes you can throw in the chives. When it's ready, on a dish you'll put the veal and pour on top the sauce. Now it's ready to serve 4 *haymisha* people. If they're on salt-free diets, leave out the pinches salt and you'll still enjoy.

* *CHERCHEZ LA FEMME*: the family plea to Howie who is 25 and still single!

PASKUDNIK POT AU FEU*

3½ lbs. beef with the bone
(for this is good *flanken*)

2½ quarts water

1 tablespoon salt

1 bouquet garni (bay leaf, pinch thyme, some pepper-corns, sprigs parsley, 1 or 2 cloves—all tied up in a cheesecloth *shmatah*)

2 chopped onions

3 carrots, quartered

1 parsnip, quartered

1 tomato, quartered

2 stalks celery

6 potatoes

The meat you'll put, along with the water, salt, and bouquet garni into a big pot. Bring it to a boil and you'll keep skimming that grey foamy stuff that keeps rising to the top. When the grey stuff doesn't rise anymore, throw in the chopped onions, the carrots, parsnip, tomato and the celery. Put on the cover and let it simmer for 4 hours. At the end of the 4 hours (if you took a nap, you'll be sure to set the alarm) put in the potatoes and let the whole thing simmer for another 45 minutes. To serve this, take from the pot the meat, put in the middle of a nice platter, and around it you'll put the large pieces of the cooked vegetables. From the broth you should skim the fat and serve as a nice soup. Or you can save it for nice stock for other recipes. (For this you'll strain.) The meat should serve at least 5 people. You'll find the meat is very good like it is and even better with:

HORSERADISH SAUCE FOR FANCY FLANKEN

1 tablespoon *parve* oleo

1½ tablespoons flour

1 cup vegetable or beef broth

Salt & pepper to taste

1 tablespoon prepared horseradish

Melt the oleo and dissolve in it the flour. Then pour in nice and slow the broth and let cook for 15 minutes. Put in the salt, pepper and horseradish. Keep heating on a low fire. Put it to the table so if the folks want horseradish on their beef, they'll have.

*PASKUDNIK: the kid who told the neighbors all about his mother's operation.

FOWL

CHICKEN SAUTÉ B'NAI B'RITH*

1–3 lb. chicken, cut up	2 tablespoons rich chicken broth
3 tablespoons *parve* oleo	1 teaspoon lemon juice
¾ cup dry white wine	1 tablespoon curaçao

A little salt

Brown nice the chicken in the oleo and then the wine you'll pour in. Put on the cover and let it cook over a low fire, oh, about 40 minutes, it should be tender. Then you can take it out from the pan and keep it warm. Pour in the pan, the broth, lemon juice, curaçao and the salt. Let this cook for a couple minutes and then over the pieces chicken you'll pour. This makes enough for 3 or 4 people and it's a very popular dish at B'nai B'rith banquets in Aix-en-Provence.

*B'NAI B'RITH: the Jewish answer to the Knights of Columbus.

SHICKER CHICKEN KIEV*

3 large chicken breasts
1 tablespoon *parve* margerine, for sautéeing
6 mushrooms, chopped very fine
½ lb. *parve* margerine, soft

1 clove garlic, mashed nice
2 tablespoons chopped parsley
Salt & pepper to taste
1 tablespoon vodka
2 eggs

Bread crumbs, very fine

Take from the chicken breasts the bones with a very sharp knife (and watch you don't leave it around where the kids'll play with it) and separate each breast in 2 halves. Put each half between wax paper and make it flat by pounding a little. Meantime you'll sauté the chopped mushrooms in about 1 tablespoon *parve* margerine. Now cream together the ½ lb. *parve* margerine, garlic, parsley and mushrooms. Chill in refrigerator, then shape it into 6 rolls about 3 inches long and 1 inch wide. Again in the refrigerator you'll put them. Now season those flat chicken breasts with salt and pepper. Place 1 cooled margerine roll on each chicken breast and roll the meat around the roll. Fold in nice the ends so the margerine roll is all inside. If you don't do this, all the margerine leaks out and there goes the Kiev in the chicken! Put toothpicks in the breasts to hold together. Now with the vodka, beat the eggs and roll the chicken in bread crumbs . . . then in the eggs . . . then in the bread crumbs again. Sauté this in plenty *parve* margerine, but not too hot, until the rolls are golden. Drain on a paper towel and put in a hot oven 400° about 5 minutes till the chicken is tender. This serves 3 people and it's so delicious you won't believe it. But with all that margerine it would be a sin to serve dessert. If your company brought some sweet stuff, you can pretend you forgot about it. Serve a little brandy and maybe they'll forget.

*SHICKER: Dean Martin at a Jewish wedding.

PUSHKEH POULET CHASSEUR*

2½-3 lbs. chicken, quartered
2 tablespoons *parve* oleo
2 shallots, minced
1 cup mushrooms
1 tablespoon flour
1 teaspoon salt
Dash pepper

½ teaspoon chervil
½ teaspoon parsley, chopped
1 can tomatoes
½ cup dry white wine
3 or 4 slices bread, fried in
  parve oleo

Season the pieces chicken so they'll have a good taste. Brown them in oleo on both sides. When that's done, remove them from the skillet and in the leftover oleo you can sauté the shallots and mushrooms. You can add a little oleo if there's none left in the pan, because now you have to sprinkle in the flour and stir till it's mixed up with any oleo left in the pan. Add the seasonings, tomatoes and wine and bring to a boil. For about 5 minutes you'll keep cooking. Now, make lower the heat and put the chicken in the sauce. Cover whatever you're cooking in and cook slowly for about 45 minutes or until the chicken is tender and looks good enough to eat. Garnish the chicken with small squares of bread you fried a healthy tan in the oleo. This chicken will have a delicious sauce you shouldn't waste. Maybe you'll make rice or potatoes or maybe you'll serve more bread on the side. Whatever you do is your business and it should make happy 4 or 5 people.

*PUSHKEH: the Jewish Chase Manhattan.

42

POULET DE LA GOYISHA PUHNIM*

3-4 lbs. quartered chicken
2 cups uncooked rice
2 onions
2 cloves garlic, minced
2 carrots, cooked

1 can peas
2 teaspoons salt
Dash pepper
½ lb. mushrooms
2 cups dry red wine

4 tablespoons *parve* oleo

Sauté the chicken in the oleo until it's a lovely golden. Then you'll take it out from what you're sautéing in and put in a good size casserole pot. Put the rice in the same frying pan and stir till it, too, is a healthy golden brown. Add the onions and garlic and sauté this nice mixture for about 10 or 15 minutes, or until the onion is soft. The frying pan had better be a good size, because now you're adding carrots, peas, salt, pepper, mushrooms and wine. Give a little stir now and then and bring the wine to a boil. Now put the whole thing in the casserole pot with the chicken. Bake it in a moderate oven—say, 350° for about 1 hour, or until the drumsticks are done. Raw chicken, nobody needs. Serve this with a big beautiful salad, a nice glass Kosher wine, it should be dry—and maybe crusty French bread. This will serve 5 to 6 people who'll need extra napkins if they pick up the chicken. And if you pick up, they'll pick up.

*GOYISHA PUHNIM: what all beautiful Jewish babies have.

43

ALTE COQ AU VIN*

1 lb. mushrooms, sliced	¼ cup flour
10 small white onions, whole	1 tablespoon parsley
3 shallots, chopped	1 bay leaf
1 clove garlic, chopped	A little salt & pepper
1 medium carrot, chopped	1½ cups dry red wine
4 tablespoons oil	2 teaspoons cornstarch mixed
1-3 lb. chicken, cut in pieces	in 2 teaspoons water

Brown first the mushrooms, onions, shallots, garlic and carrot in half of the oil. Then you can take out from the pan. Now dredge good the chicken in the flour and throw in the rest of the oil into the pan. Brown the chicken in this all over. Put back the vegetables and add the parsley, bay leaf, salt, pepper, and wine. Cover the pan and you'll cook for 1 hour on a very low flame. Just before it's ready, mix in the cornstarch mixture and let it cook for another 2 or 3 minutes. This will make the sauce just thick enough so it should stick to the rice you can serve it with. It makes enough for 4 people and a sauce you'll take pleasure dunking in the next day.

*ALTE: when she walks into the room on Shabbos, all the smokers develop cupped hands.

44

CHICKEN LIVERS DE MA TANTE ROSE*

1 lb. chicken livers
3 tablespoons *parve* oleo
½ lb. sliced mushrooms

1½ tablespoons flour
½ cup rich beef stock
½ cup dry red wine

A little salt & pepper

Salt and broil the livers a little bit on each side, so they should be Kosher. Rinse off from them the salt and in the melted oleo, you'll sauté the livers for about 2 minutes. Put in next the mushrooms and flour and for another 3 minutes you'll sauté and stir so the flour gets nice and brown. Now pour in the rich beef stock and wine and sprinkle in a little salt and pepper so your food should have a nice flavor. Put a cover on the pan and you'll simmer everything together for about 15 minutes. If you serve this on rice, the rice will soak up all that good gravy. This is a healthy dish with lots of nourishment; and if you tell the kids there's wine cooked in, they'll be glad to eat the livers. Serves 3 or 4 iron-starved kids.

* *MA TANTE ROSE:* when you were a kid, she's the one who always said, "You're too pale! Your mother should give you some iron!"

DUCK EN GELÉE À LA
GUILLOTINE*

1 4-5 lb. duckling	1 envelope Kosher gelatin,
2 carrots, skinny	unflavored
1 onion	1 egg shell, crumpled up
1 tablespoon parsley	1 teaspoon salt
1 bay leaf	¼ teaspoon white pepper
1 cup dry red wine	½ cup pitted black olives
1 egg white	1 egg, hard-boiled

Simmer good the duck together with the carrots and onion in
about a quart of water. Do this in a covered pot for an hour and
a half so it'll be tender, the duck. When it's ready, take the
duck out from the broth and remove first the skin. This you'll
save. Next you'll remove the meat from the bones. This you'll
also save. Then you'll skim the broth and *save the fat*. Now
put the bones back into the broth and put in also the parsley,
bay leaf and red wine. Let this cook on the back of the stove
without a cover until it steams down to 2 cups. While you're
steaming, you can also fry. Cut up the skin into small pieces
and fry it in some of the fat you skimmed a few minutes ago.
Do this until they're brown and crisp like a potato chip. Then

you can drain and put them aside. And don't nibble! Now stir up the egg white and a crumpled egg shell and throw this mess into the broth. Let it simmer for a few minutes and you'll see how the broth clears. Next you can strain this whole thing through a clean cloth. Mix up the gelatin in a little water and heat it until it melts good. Then throw it into the broth and mix it in. Also mix in the salt and pepper. Now you'll pour enough of this liquid into an 11" x 5" x 3" loaf pan so the bottom gets covered. Put the pan into the refrigerator for a few minutes to set. Then put in a layer duck slices, a layer crisp skin, a layer olives, a layer sliced hard-boiled egg, the 2 whole skinny carrots from before, and another layer duck meat. Pour over this the rest of the liquid and put on top a piece wood for a weight to press it nice. Now the whole thing you should put into the refrigerator and let it chill overnight. To serve, you'll dip the pan into hot water for a few minutes and then turn it upside down on a serving platter. It'll plop right out. Slice it up into slices with a VERY sharp knife and be very careful it shouldn't fall apart. Now it's ready to serve for a cold lunch that'll be so exciting, everybody will be jealous. Serves 5 or 6 hungry, jealous people.

*GUILLOTINE: a dangerous weapon in the hands of the wrong mohel.

FAHSHLUGENUH DUCK FLAMBÉ*

1-5 lb. duck   ½ teaspoon salt
3 cups water

FOR THE ORANGE SAUCE, YOU'LL NEED:

1 tablespoon sugar   2 teaspoons cornstarch
1 tablespoon vinegar   ¾ cup orange juice
                    4 tablespoons brandy

In a covered pot you'll cook good the duck in the salted water for 1 hour. This gets rid of all that extra fat so you should have a healthy gall bladder. Now put the duck into a 425° oven for 45 minutes to finish cooking it to a nice color brown. While you're in the oven, you can skim from the broth the fat. Put aside 1 cup of this broth for the sauce and put the rest into the refrigerator for some other day. Take 1 tablespoon sugar and the vinegar and heat them together in a small pot until the color changes to a dark brown. While you're doing this you can also put into another pot 1 cup of the broth and the cornstarch dissolved in a little water. Heat this and stir it up good until it gets thickened. Then you can throw in the orange juice and the browned caramelized sugar. If it needs, you can throw in a little more sugar. Cook this on a low fire for 5 minutes. When it's almost done, comes the best part. Pour in 2 tablespoons brandy! Ooh, is this going to be a sauce! When the duck is done, into serving pieces you'll cut. Just before you're ready to serve, pour over it the rest of the brandy, a little warmed up, and set it on fire. Serve this with the sauce on the side, so everyone can take what they want. This is enough for 4 people who better eat fast before the Fire Department comes.

*FAHSHLUGENUH: the "helpful" neighbor who gave you a cutting of ivy for the garden and it turned out to be the itchy kind

FISH

TROUT AMANDINE QVETCH
DE MAMAN*

2 lbs. of trout filets   ½ cup slivered almonds
1 egg, beaten   2 tablespoons lemon juice
¼ cup milk   1 teaspoon Worcestershire Sauce
Flour to dredge   1 tablespoon chopped parsley
½ cup butter   Salt & pepper, you'll be generous

Season good the trout with the salt and pepper. Beat up the egg together with the milk and dip in it each piece trout. Then you'll dredge each piece in the flour. ("Dredge" for new brides means to cover the trout with the flour, or you can call your mother-in-law and ask her. She'll be thrilled.) Melt the butter in a frying pan and sauté on both sides the trout until it's nice and brown. Now you'll put it on a warm platter. Put in the frying pan with the leftover butter the almonds, and you'll brown them a little. Add then the lemon juice, Worcestershire Sauce and parsley and warm everything together. Pour this over the trout and it'll make 3 or 4 nice servings. This is a good way to get the kids to eat fish . . . they'll love chewing on those tasty almonds. If you're a new bride, you should ignore that last sentence. If it applies to you anyway, for shame!

*QVETCH DE MAMAN: "I only hope when you have a daughter she talks to you the same way!"

50

FAHPITZT FILET OF SOLE
MEUNIÈRE

6 filets of sole	¼ cup vegetable oil
1 teaspoon salt	4 tablespoons butter
A good pinch pepper	A little lemon juice
¼ cup flour	A little chopped parsley

Wash very good the filets and pat them dry with a paper towel. Mix together the salt, pepper and flour and dust the filets all over. Heat very hot the oil in a frying pan (be sure it's big enough for all the filets) and cook on both sides the fish until they're a lovely golden color, you should be proud! Take them out, drain them to remove the extra oil and put on a warm serving plate. (How you'll get it warm is your problem.) Throw away the oil that's in the frying pan. (If you pour it down the sink, be sure to run the hot water at the same time.) Now, you'll put the butter in the frying pan and let it get brown. Pour the browned butter over the filets, sprinkle on a little lemon juice and parsley and it's a dish fit for a King. Serves 4 to 5 Kings, depending on the size of the filets and the size of the Kings.

FAHPITZT: describes the "ladies" of Place Pigalle who are the self appointed Welcome Wagon of Paris.

51

COQUILLE DE MON FRÈRE JACQUES*

3 cups cubed halibut	1 tablespoon butter
1 cup dry white wine	3 tablespoons water
1 cup water	2 tablespoons lemon juice
A pinch thyme	⅛ teaspoon pepper
A couple sprigs parsley	2 tablespoons flour
A small bay leaf	1 teaspoon salt
1 celery stalk	2 egg yolks
½ lb. chopped mushrooms	3 tablespoons heavy cream
½ cup chopped scallions	2 tablespoons Parmesan cheese,
1 tablespoon chopped parsley	grated

Enough butter so you can dot

Put the halibut cubes in with the wine, 1 cup water, thyme, the sprigs parsley, bay leaf and the celery in your favorite big pot. Bring it to a boil till it sounds like it might explode, and then you'll lower the fire and cook for another 10 minutes. Take out from this the fish. So you shouldn't burn yourself, use a tablespoon with slots if you have. Put the fish aside and strain the stock and put it back into the nice pot. Throw away the strained stuff, you won't need it anymore. Now boil the stock again until you have only about a cup and a half left. If you're familiar with your own pot, you should know where a cup and a half will be on it. If it's not exact, nobody'll be hurt. Meantime, in another pot, maybe a saucepan, you'll put the mushrooms, scallions, chopped parsley, butter, 3 tablespoons water, lemon juice and pepper. Cover it and cook it on a low fire for 10 minutes. Now you'll stir in the flour and salt and very slowly you'll pour in the cup and a half stock you cooked. Cook it a couple minutes, but don't stop stirring. Turn off now the fire so everything will cool a little bit. In a bowl, beat up the egg yolks with the cream and then slowly pour in the mushroom mish-mash you were cooking in the saucepan. While you're pouring, you should keep stirring. Those pieces halibut that have been standing by you can put in now. Divide this mixture into 6 ovenproof individual serving dishes. Sprinkle on the top the Parmesan cheese, and here and there you'll make a dot with the butter. Stick these 6 dishes under the broiler so they can brown on top, serve and sit back and wait for the compliments. If you don't get any, then you didn't follow the recipe.

* MON FRÈRE JACQUES: my rotten brother Jack who married my old girlfriend and now she's my sister-in-law!

53

KING SOLOMON'S SALMON
MAYONNAISE*

FIRST, YOU'LL MAKE TAKEH A MAYONNAISE:

2 egg yolks	2 tablespoons tarragon vinegar
1 cup salad oil	1 tablespoon parsley, chopped
½ teaspoon salt	1 clove garlic, minced
¼ teaspoon pepper	½ teaspoon dry mustard

It's sometimes easier if you start with the yolks and oil at room temperature, but it's not absolutely a must. Put the yolks into a mixing bowl, and add salt, and pepper and you'll stir and stir. (In this recipe you never stop with the stirring.) Pour in the oil *very* slowly, drop by drop. If you don't, you'll get one big mess! Keep stirring, keep adding oil, stirring, pouring, until the oil is all poured in and the sauce is thick. Now you'll add vinegar, parsley, garlic, and mustard and stir it all to mix nice.

If the sauce separates, you shouldn't get upset. Don't throw the whole thing out. Just put 1 fresh egg yolk in another bowl and little by little, add the old separated mixture.

If you think you'll keep the mayonnaise a few days, add 1 tablespoon boiling water after it's mixed.

This mayonnaise is not like the store-bought stuff. And if

you don't have the patience to make this kind to serve with your salmon, then close the book and cook TV dinners. And don't be surprised if you'll get hurt looks from that lovely family of yours.

Makes about 2 cups for happy families.

NOW, FOR THE SALMON:

3-7 oz. cans salmon
Shredded lettuce

You'll garnish attractive the bottom of a salad bowl with seasoned shredded lettuce. Smash up the salmon, you'll make sure to remove the skins and bones carefully. Put the salmon on top of the lettuce, spread lots of that tasty mayonnaise on top the salmon and decorate with capers, anchovies, radishes, hardboiled egg slices—anything you think makes nice decoration. The mayonnaise that's left over is wonderful as a sandwich spread. This dish is very nice to eat on *Shabbos* and is a nice change from cold cuts. Serves 4 to 6 people who don't mind smelling from garlic.

*KING SOLOMON: the first marriage counsellor in Jerusalem; had 300 wives and was considered a real *mayvin*.

BEI MIR BIST DU SHÖN
BOUILLABAISE*

4 lbs. various Kosher fish filets cut in 2-inch pieces
A few fish heads and bones
A good pinch thyme
1 tablespoon lemon juice
3 bay leaves
A few sprigs parsley
1½ quarts water
2 nice size onions, chopped fine

4 minced up cloves garlic
3 tablespoons oil
2 tablespoons flour
2 cups tomato sauce
2 teaspoons powdered allspice
Enough salt for a taste
A few sprinkles cayenne pepper
A good pinch saffron
½ cup dry white wine

Put the fish heads and the bones together with the thyme, lemon juice, bay leaves and parsley into the pot water. Let it boil good for about 10 minutes without a cover. Don't get worried if some of it disappears . . . it's supposed to. While you're boiling you'll sauté until it's nice and soft, the onions and garlic in the oil. Throw in the flour, it should get nice and brown (this by the French is called a "roux"). By now everything that was boiling should be boiled, so you'll strain the liquid very carefully and throw the other stuff away. Who needs old fish heads and bones and cooked-out spices? Now be sure the liquid is in a big pot . . . and to this you'll add the sautéed onions and garlic and the "roux." Throw in the tomato sauce, allspice, salt, pepper, saffron and the wine. Give a nice stir, and boil everything uncovered for 5 minutes. Put in gently the pieces fish (up to now you've been throwing) . . . put on the cover and let it boil not too fast for 15 minutes.

When you're ready to serve, put a slice or two of toast or thick French bread or even a small mound of cooked rice into each big soup bowl. Put a couple pieces fish in each bowl and then spoon in lots of the soup, which by now should be a nice burnt orange color . . . unless maybe the lighting in my kitchen is different from yours. This is a one-dish meal, you should serve salad with it, and it serves about 5 fish eaters. The aroma from this dish cooking will delight your family, friends and neighborhood cats.

* BEI MIR BIST DU SHÖN: I didn't see anything wrong with your old nose.

57

FLOUNDER À LA MOISHE PIPPIK*

FOR THE MOISHE PIPPIK SAUCE, YOU'LL NEED:

1 medium onion, chopped
1 tablespoon butter
¾ cup drained canned
    tomatoes, chopped up
½ cup dry red wine
2 teaspoons flour
2 tablespoons chopped parsley
A pinch salt

A good pinch pepper, live it up!

First you'll make the sauce so it can simmer while the fish, it cooks. Sauté the onion in the butter until it's soft. Put the onions in a saucepan together with the tomatoes, wine, flour, parsley, salt and pepper and let it simmer for about 15 minutes, it should get thick. Every now and then you'll give a stir.

PREPARE NOW THE FLOUNDER:

6 flounder filets
Salt & pepper for flavoring
½ cup milk
2 eggs, beaten up
½ cup flour
1 cup bread crumbs

1 cup oil

Season the fish very good with salt and pepper. Mix the milk with the egg and dip each filet into the flour, then the egg-mixture, then the bread crumbs. Be very generous with the bread crumbs. Heat the oil in a good size frying pan and fry each filet until it's golden brown on both sides.

When the fish are done, you'll drain them on paper towels or maybe brown paper if you have. On separate plates, you can put a bed of sauce, then the filets go on top the sauce to serve 4 to 6 people. With this meal you should serve a glass wine and you should propose a toast to the man responsible for this dish . . . Count Moishe Pippik!

MOISHE PIPPIK: the famous swashbuckler known to millions as the Count of Monte Cristo.

VEGETABLES

GREEN PEAS TATTELUH
AU TARRAGON*

1 can young spring peas	½ teaspoon MSG
¼ teaspoon dry tarragon	2 teaspoons *parve* oleo
Salt & pepper to taste	2 teaspoons flour

When you open the can peas, pour off half the liquid . . . not all, because you'll make good use of what's left. Now, the peas and the liquid you didn't throw away you'll throw into a saucepan along with the tarragon, salt, pepper and MSG. Cook everything on a low fire until it's nice and heated up. While this is heating, you'll make a *beurre manié*, which don't let the fancy name scare you. The oleo and flour you should knead together so it makes a smooth round ball. Then after you went to all that trouble to make it into one ball, you'll break it up into lots of little pea-size balls. When the peas are hot enough to serve, drop in the little balls of *beurre manié* and stir until they dissolve and the pea juice thickens. This makes, for 5 to 6 people, the most delicious peas you ever had. From this you'll never get thin, but you'll be a happy "heavy."

*TATTELUH: a term of endearment given to little boys before they're old enough to do anything about it.

GREEN PEAS À LA PLACE
DE LA CONCORD*

2 cups shelled peas
10 leaves of lettuce, shredded
8 small white onions
A pinch basil

A pinch salt
4 tablespoons butter
A sprig parsley
¼ cup water

2 teaspoons flour

In a saucepan you'll dump the peas, the lettuce, the onions, the basil, salt, 3 tablespoons butter, parsley and water. Then you'll put on the cover and cook for about 20 minutes until they're tender. While you're cooking you can make a *beurre manié* with the tablespoon of butter that's left and the flour. (This you'll do by kneading together the flour and butter until they're nice and soft.) When the peas are done, you'll break the *beurre manié* into small bits and sprinkle them around on the peas. Give the pan a couple good shakes back and forth so the *beurre manié* can dissolve and make the pea juice nice and thick. And that's all there is to it. You can always use canned peas or frozen peas. But it brings back a lot of memories when you sit and shell peas . . . and it's fun for the kids to do when they're home from school. If you're eating *fleischig* you'll use *parve* oleo instead of butter, it'll be just as good. Serves 5 pea lovers.

*CONCORD: the Jewish Pentagon in the Catskills.

61

EPPES EGGPLANT AUX FINES HERBES*

1 medium eggplant	2 chopped shallots
¼ cup *parve* oleo	1 tablespoon chopped parsley
1 chopped onion	1 tablespoon chopped chives
2 cloves garlic, chopped	½ teaspoon marjoram
	Salt & pepper for tasting

Slice the eggplant into ½ inch slices and into boiling water you should put them for 3 minutes. Meanwhile, sauté in the oleo the onion, garlic, shallots, parsley, chives, marjoram, salt and pepper. Do this until they're nice and soft. Now take out from the water the slices eggplant and drain them. Then you can put them into a greased baking dish. Smear on each piece eggplant a little of the sautéed mish-mash and put them into a 350° oven for 30 minutes. This makes just enough for 3 or 4 people. Or maybe even just 2 people if they really go crazy when they eat eggplant.

*HERB: in French it's the touch that puts the *haute* in *Haute Cuisine;* in Jewish it's a nice name for a fine Jewish boy.

SA DRAITA ASPARAGUS POLONAISE*

2 lbs. bunch asparagus	4 tablespoons *parve* oleo
1 hard-boiled egg, chopped	A little salt & pepper
¼ cup bread crumbs	1 tablespoon chopped parsley

Clean and trim good the asparagus and then tie the bunch together with a little string. Put it standing up in a deep pot with about 2 inches salted water in the bottom. On this you'll put a cover and let it steam on a low fire for 15 minutes so they should be tender. If they're still not tender, you'll steam a little more. When they're done, untie them and on a plate you'll put them. Sprinkle on the chopped egg. Now put the bread crumbs in a pan with the oleo, salt and pepper. Stir it up a little and let it brown good. When this is ready you'll pour it on the asparagus. Next the parsley you should sprinkle on and it's ready to serve 6 pianists who'll play rhapsodies for this dish.

*SA DRAITA: he thought *tour de force* was a ·guided tour of missile bases.

HOK IN DUH KUPP KIDNEY
BEANS AU VIN ROUGE*

2 cups dried red kidney beans	2 tablespoons *parve* oleo
1 bay leaf	1 small onion, grated
A medium pinch thyme	2 mashed garlic cloves
A few sprigs parsley	2 tablespoons flour
1 stalk celery	A healthy pinch salt
1 small envelope vegetable bouillon	A not-so-healthy pinch pepper
	1 cup dry red wine

Soak the beans overnight with enough water so it should cover. The next day you'll simmer the beans in that same water . . . but first you'll add the bay leaf, thyme, parsley, celery, and you'll sprinkle in the bouillon. Simmer all this for 2 hours.

Meantime, about 10 minutes before the beans are done, sauté in the oleo the onion and garlic. Add next the flour, salt and pepper and stir it around until it's nice and smooth. Pour in easy the wine and let this whole thing cook with a medium fire while you stir and it thickens.

When the beans are simmered, the beans you'll drain and then throw away the water with all that stuff that cooked in it. Don't make a mistake and throw away the beans. It would be very embarrassing if the neighbors knew.

Pour the wine-mixture on top of the beans and serve in a colorful casserole pot. The *goyem* almost always cook pork fat with kidney beans. This recipe just goes to show you, kidney beans can live very nicely without all that *hahzarye.*

HOK IN DUH KUPP: what Seymour got when the girl he picked up in Paris turned out to be a boy . . . . .

BROCCOLI YENTUH
TILLEBENDUH*

3 lbs. broccoli
½ cup butter or *parve* oleo
4 tablespoons lemon juice
1 smashed garlic clove

A little pinch marjoram
A good pinch salt
A nice grind of black pepper

Cut off from the broccoli all that heavy, coarse stuff on the ends . . . who needs it! Wash the broccoli good and put it in a pot with a little salted water in the bottom. Don't drown it— you only want it should steam for about 20 minutes or until it's good and tender. Melt the butter or the oleo (it depends what you'll serve the broccoli with) in a little saucepan and then throw in the rest of the stuff. When it's all mixed together you can pour it on the cooked broccoli and serve. The broccoli shouldn't be so cooked it can fall apart . . . but on the other hand, it shouldn't break your teeth either. You can test the ends with a fork now and then. This is a nice vegetable for 6 people, who, if they don't appreciate good food, won't like this dish.

YENTUH TILLEBENDUH: a concierge who works for free.

STARCHES

POTATOES RISSOLE À LA SAMSON'S TZURRIS*

4 medium potatoes   Salt & pepper, to taste
4 tablespoons butter   1 tablespoon parsley

Peel carefully the potatoes and with a fruit scooper (if you don't have one, you'll borrow from the lady next door) scoop out into little balls. Put the balls into a pot with salted water enough to cover and boil it for 8 minutes. When it's boiled, drain the potatoes, but make sure all that steam doesn't burn you. Melt 2 tablespoons butter in a large frying pan and brown half the potatoes—all of them won't fit. Take out from the pan the potatoes and put them aside somewhere not far away. Now you can melt 2 more tablespoons butter and brown the rest of the potatoes. Next you'll put all the potatoes together in a nice looking casserole, sprinkle on salt, pepper and parsley, and warm it in a 250° oven. This will make enough for 4 people who might think you got those round potatoes from a can, until you tell them you scooped.

*SAMSON'S TZURRIS: his girlfriend Delilah gave him such a haircut, it went down in history.

POTATO SOUFFLÉ OY VAY!*

2 cups mashed potatoes
¾ cup light cream
A couple pinches salt

A pinch pepper
2 egg yolks
4 egg whites

First of all your mashed potatoes should be warm. (You can use instant potatoes if you're lazy, or the other kind . . . you choose.) Now the cream you'll mix in together very good with the salt, pepper and egg yolks. With a beater you'll beat the egg whites until they're so stiff they're practically saluting. Then you'll fold the whites into the potato mixture. Put the whole thing into a casserole pot you greased first, and bake it in an oven that says 375°, for a half hour. The soufflé you'll find will get nice and brown on top and it'll rise. Serve it right away when it's done and keep talking so your guests shouldn't notice that it settles down a little as it cools. Serves 4 or 5 talking guests.

*OY VAY!: Grandma's shock when the Paris "hotel" she went into to use the lady's room turned out to be the Egyptian Embassy.

68

MARVIN'S POMMES DE TERRE
À SAVOIR FAIRE*

4 large potatoes, peeled
  & sliced thin
1 teaspoon salt
A few sprinkles black pepper

2 cups milk
1 tablespoon butter
½ cup heavy cream

¼ cup grated Parmesan cheese

Put the potatoes, salt and pepper together with the milk in a double boiler. Let it cook a half hour, you'll be sure it's covered. Now you'll shmear well a baking dish with 1 tablespoon of butter and put the potato-milk mixture in it. Over this you'll pour the cream, then sprinkle on the Parmesan cheese. Put the whole thing uncovered into a 350° oven for 25 minutes so the top, it gets browned. This dish is very good to help 6 undernourished people get some meat on their bones, or serves 5 people who don't care how much meat they get on their bones.

*MARVIN'S SAVIOR FAIRE: when the newlyweds told him they were expecting, he counted the months on his fingers behind his back.

69

MITTEN DE RINNIN RICE
AUX CHAMPIGNONS*

2 tablespoons *parve* oleo
1 medium onion, chopped
1 cup sliced mushrooms
1 cup rice
2 cups nice chicken broth
A good pinch salt

Melt first the oleo and in it you'll put the onion and mushrooms and cook until the onions are nice and soft. Next you'll dump in the rice and mix everything all together. While you're mixing, you should also boil the chicken broth and the salt. Then over the rice you'll pour the boiling broth, put on the pot the cover, and cook on a low fire for 20 minutes. If it comes out maybe a little dry, you'll sprinkle on a little more broth. To make this dish good, be sure you have nice rice that isn't all stuck together. If it is, don't tell them where you got the recipe. That kind of business, who needs? Serves 3 to 4 champions.

*MITTEN DE RINNIN: you're on the front row half way through a Broadway play, and Bobby whispers he has to "go" . . .

DESSERTS

BLINTZ SUZETTE*

This dish, like Gaul, is divided in three parts:

FIRST, THERE'S THE BATTER:

1 cup sifted flour	1 cup milk
A good pinch salt	4 nice fresh eggs, beaten up

Sift together the flour with the salt. Then you can mix up the milk and eggs with it. For this a blender is good. Now take a 6 inch pan and shmear in it a little butter. Pour some batter in the pan and tilt it around a little so it gets spread out nice. If you don't pour too much batter and you tilt good the pan, the cake will be nice and thin. Cook on a low fire until the top gets a little dry. Then it's done. Take it out from the pan and on a cloth or a napkin you'll put it to cool. Keep doing this until you're all used up.

NOW COMES THE FILLING:

1 lb. nice dry cottage cheese	1 tablespoon melted butter
1 beaten egg yolk	3 tablespoons sugar
	A pinch salt

72

Mix good together all this stuff. Now taste it. If you like a little sweeter, put in more sugar. Now you can divide a little of this on each cake. Fold the cake like an envelope (or like a blintz). After this, into a greased pan you'll put them and bake them nice in a 350° oven for 20 minutes.

AND LAST, BUT NOT LEAST, THE SAUCE:

½ cup butter	1 teaspoon lemon juice
½ cup powdered sugar	¼ cup orange juice
¼ teaspoon dried orange peel	¼ cup curaçao

Melt together with the butter, the sugar. Then put in the orange peel, lemon juice, orange juice, and curaçao. Mix it all together nice and some of this you'll pour on each serving blintzes. Then on each serving you'll also pour a little brandy. This you can set on fire and serve right away, you shouldn't burn yourself. You'll have enough to serve 4 people 2 blintzes each, with maybe a blintz or two left over, which you can eat like a sneak in the kitchen while you're doing the dishes. Such a *hahzar!*

* *BLINTZ*: a crêpe with a superiority complex.

73

BUBBA AU RHUM*

FOR THE CAKE PART, YOU'LL NEED:

2 cups flour	A pinch salt
1 envelope yeast	1 tablespoon sugar
½ cup warm water	1 tablespoon raisins
4 eggs, beaten	1 tablespoon dry currants
¼ cup butter	1 teaspoon grated lemon rind

Sift first the flour and then dissolve the yeast in the warm water and pour it on the flour, which let's hope is in a bowl. Now add the eggs and with your hands you'll squish around until the dough is like rubber. Next, mix in good the butter. Cover up the bowl of dough with a cloth, it should be clean, and put it in a warm place to rise until it's twice as big. This should take maybe 1½ hours. Now you can punch down the dough and work in the salt, the sugar, raisins, currants, and lemon rind. You'll work out a lot of frustrations when you play with this dough. If you don't have a fancy mold for this (like I don't), you can use even a 12 muffin muffin-tin, it's just as good. Grease very nice the muffin-tin and you'll put the dough in the 12 holes, the same amount in each one. Each hole or mold should be maybe ⅔ full and don't worry if the top doesn't look so smooth . . . it'll smooth by itself. Put the molds or the muffin-tin in that warm place you used before for the bowl of dough and let it rise until all the cakes are about ¼ inch above the top. This should take maybe a half hour. Then put the muffin-tin or molds in a 425° oven, and bake for 15 minutes. When you stick in a toothpick, it should come out clean. When they're done, lift them out from the tin or the molds and put them aside; you're not finished yet.

NOW FOR THE BEST PART—THE "RHUM" PART:

2 cups water
1 cup sugar
⅔ cup rum

Together you'll boil the water and sugar until you have a clear syrup. Then mix in the rum. With a skewer you'll poke lots of holes in the çakes and you'll arrange them in a deep dish and pour over them the rum syrup. Your kitchen might smell a little like the Bowery, but with class! Let them sit like this for ½ hour and every now and then you'll give another baste. Then drain them for maybe 15 minutes.

AND, FINALLY, HERE IS A GLAZE TO SCHMALTZ UP THE WHOLE THING:

3 tablespoons apricot preserves
2 tablespoons water

Put the preserves and water together in a saucepan. Heat and stir until it's nice and smooth. Now with a little brush you'll paint the top of each cake to make a nice glaze, put them in the refrigerator and you'll later have a dessert to serve nobody'll believe you made. Serves 12 *bubbas* who'll be very happy to eat a dessert named after them. And it wouldn't be a bad idea you should give them also a copy of this book, they'll have their own recipe.

* *BUBBA AU RHUM*: Grandma after her first nightclub visit!

TOUT DE SUITE STRAWBERRIES
AVEC COGNAC*

1 quart of strawberries
½ cup sugar
⅓ cup cognac

6 slices sponge cake, already
made

If you don't have a quart to measure the strawberries, you'll find 2 baskets of strawberries make 1 quart. Wash carefully the strawberries and take off from them the green things. Put in a big bowl the cleaned up strawberries and sprinkle on all over the sugar. Put it in the refrigerator for about an hour so they'll be cold. Every now and then you'll stroll in and give a stir and maybe steal a berry. When you're ready to serve, pour over it the cognac. In 6 plates you'll put a slice of sponge cake —you can get the recipe from Jennie Grossinger's book—dish out the berries over the slices cake and pour the extra juice on, too. This is a nice dessert for 6 people, if you didn't steal too many berries when you were chilling.

*TOUT DE SUITE: refers to Shelly's wedding after her summer in the Catskills.

PEARS FOLIES BERGÈRE*

6 fresh pears
½ cup dry red wine
1 small piece lemon peel

1 cup sugar
1 small stick cinnamon

First you should peel the pears, cut them in half and take out from them the cores. In a saucepan you'll mix together the wine, sugar, cinnamon, and lemon peel. Bring this to a nice, healthy boil and cook a few pear halves at a time until they're soft. (If all 12 halves fit in your pot, you've got some pot!) Now take out from the syrup the cinnamon and lemon peel and cook the liquid until only about half of it is left. Pour this over the pears and put them in the refrigerator, they should be served cold enough to hurt the fillings in the teeth. Serves 6 people whose class had fewer cavities.

* FOLIES BERGÈRE: France's answer to the Hadassah Chanukah skit.

TZIMMIS DE FRUITE FLAMBÉ*

2 lbs. of dried fruits   1 cup water
  (apricots, prunes, raisins)   ½ cup rice
1 cup orange juice   2 tablespoons curaçao
2 teaspoons sugar   ½ cup brandy

Wash the fruit carefully and drain it nice, it should be dry. Put it aside for a few minutes, and bring the orange juice, sugar and water to a boil in a pretty casserole pot. Add next the fruit and rice, you'll simmer in the casserole for 20 minutes, and make sure it's covered. When the rice is tender, and stir once in awhile so it doesn't stick, stir in the curaçao and sprinkle on the brandy and bring it to the table. (Now you see why the casserole should be pretty . . . because everybody has to look at it.) Turn off the lights and hurry, before everyone gets scared, and light the brandy. This will light up 6 people.

* *TZIMMIS:* what Murray's wife made when he overtipped the French maid.

POTCHKUH MOUSSE AU CHOCOLAT*

2 1-oz. squares of semi-
    sweet chocolate
½ cup water
1 tablespoon unflavored
    Kosher gelatin
¼ cup cold water

3 egg yolks
2 tablespoons sugar
A pinch salt
1 tablespoon curaçao
1 tablespoon sugar
3 egg whites

Melt the chocolate in the ½ cup water on a low fire. While you're melting, the gelatin you'll soften in the ¼ cup cold water and then mix it into the chocolate. Beat now the egg yolks together with the 2 tablespoons sugar and this, too, you'll pour into the chocolate stuff along with the salt and the curaçao. (Curaçao is used so much in this book, you'd better run out and buy some for the house. Besides it looks good in the kitchen.) Now into a dry clean bowl—and, believe me, it better be dry—dump the egg whites and another pinch salt and with a dry beater, you'll beat like crazy until the egg whites make like little peaks. (So many mousses I had to make to do this recipe! So you don't be smart and try short cuts.) Now add the 1 tablespoon sugar to the beaten egg whites and again you'll beat until it's so stiff, if you put a whole egg on top, it wouldn't sink. (I'm not joking . . . that's how stiff you have to be.) Take a big spoonful of the beaten whites and mix it in with the chocolate mixture. Now put the rest of the beaten whites on top the chocolate mixture and fold in very gently with a spatula. If all the white doesn't mix in too well . . . that's all right, too. Because if you don't fold gently, you might push from the egg whites too much air . . . and then you'll have a mashed mousse. Put the bowl in the refrigerator to chill good for a few hours and then you can serve about 6 people who, let's hope, they didn't bring over their own dessert.

*POTCHKUH: what kids do when they look for the chocolate with the cherry in the middle.

QUELLE HEURE EST-IL CAFÉ.
AU LAIT?*

For this kind coffee you should use a porcelain coffee pot instead of an aluminum pot which will only get black from the water, sooner or later.

Ahead of time, you can make a very strong coffee they call *café noir*, which is no small coincidence, it means black coffee. (Those nice smart Frenchmen think of everything.) You boil some water and first you'll rinse out the basket and the lower half of the coffee pot with a little of the water. Don't ask why —but a real coffee maker *mayvin* does this; so you don't ask questions, just do. Then fill the basket with coffee. Now some people say you should use 1 tablespoon coffee for each tablespoon water . . . but this will give you such a strong coffee, you'll have hair on your chest! So you may have to try a few times and see how strong you like it. In my pot I use 8 tablespoons coffee and 2 cups boiling water. Now slowly, you'll pour over the coffee the boiling water, until it's all used up. When it's all through dripping into the bottom of the pot, you'll put the *café noir* in a jar and refrigerate until you need it, or you can take a little and have a cup coffee right now. You can make all you want, and just heat it up every time you want some. This isn't like the usual coffee you have to have fresh every time.

To make the CAFÉ AU LAIT, which it turns out is a very weak and very tasty French coffee, you heat up the *café noir* (never boil it; just heat it) and put a little in each coffee cup —say, about ⅓ or ½ full. And then you'll pour very hot milk to the top of the cup.

This the French always have after a *milchig* meal. It takes a little more time than the usual type of coffee, but you won't get as nervous.

*QUELLE HEURE EST-IL? this is the longest sermon he's ever made!

80

INDEX

82